MURTY CLASSICAL
LIBRARY OF INDIA

THE RISALO
OF SHAH ABDUL LATIF

SHAH ABDUL LATIF

THE RISALO OF SHAH ABDUL LATIF

Sufi Poetry from Sindh

Translated by
CHRISTOPHER SHACKLE

MURTY CLASSICAL LIBRARY OF INDIA
HARVARD UNIVERSITY PRESS
Cambridge, Massachusetts
London, England
2025

Printed in the United States of America
First printing

First published in Murty Classical Library of India,
Volume 18, Harvard University Press, 2018.

SERIES DESIGN BY M9DESIGN
TYPESETTING BY TITUS NEMETH

Library of Congress Cataloging-in-Publication Data

Names: ʻAbd al-Laṭīf, Shah, approximately 1689-approximately 1752, author. | Shackle, C., translator.
Title: The risalo of Shah Abdul Latif : Sufi poetry from Sindh / Shah Abdul Latif ; translated by Christopher Shackle.
Other titles: Murty classical library of India.
Description: Cambridge, Massachusetts ; London, England : Harvard University Press, 2025. | Series: Murty classical library of india | This is an English only edition of Risalo by Shah Abdul Latif, published by Havard University Press in 2018. The Sindhi text has been taken out and the introduction has been slightly edited. | Includes bibliographical references.
Identifiers: LCCN 2025020105 | ISBN 9780674302822 (paperback) | ISBN 9780674303751 (pdf) | ISBN 9780674303744 (epub)
Subjects: LCSH: Sindhi poetry—Translations into English. | LCGFT: Poetry.
Classification: LCC PK2788.9.A2 R513 2025 | DDC 891.4/113—dc23/eng/20250625
LC record available at https://lccn.loc.gov/2025020105

EU GPSR Authorised Representative
Logos Europe, 9 rue Nicolas Poussin, 17000, La Rochelle, France
Contact@logoseurope.eu

CONTENTS

INTRODUCTION

The Life

The *Risālo* is a large collection of Sindhi lyrical poetry by the eighteenth-century Sufi poet Shah Abdul Latif (1689–1752) of Bhit, near Hyderabad in modern-day Pakistan.[1] It is one of the greatest works of Sufi poetry in a South Asian language, and is universally acknowledged to be the greatest classic of Sindhi literature in both Sindh itself and other parts of Pakistan, as well as among the Sindhi émigré population in India and the wider diaspora.

The Sindhi word *Risālo* is the title always given to Shah Latif's collected poetry. It derives from the Arabic *risāla* "treatise" (typically one written on an Islamic topic, often in prose), which is itself cognate with the word *rasūl* "apostle" used as a title of the prophet Muhammad. The common loose translation of *Risālo* as "the Message" thus conveys an appropriate sense of the poetry's uniquely inspired character. *Risālo* employs the full resources of the Sindhi language to present a uniquely vivid and varied expression of the central Sufi understanding of the created world as a direct manifestation of the divine, and of love as the all-powerful force that connects God with his creatures.

Shah Latif belonged to one of the many lineages of hereditary Sufi saints established in the countryside of Sindh, where they have always enjoyed great prestige and power as *pīrs* or holy men with a special spiritual authority. The honorific title Shah indicates his status as a Sayyid claiming direct descent from the prophet Muhammad. The largely hagiographic accounts of his life are of the usual limited use in constructing a fully detailed biography. It appears that unlike many of the *pīrs* of Sindh or leading Sufis in other parts of South Asia, he was not formally affiliated in a chain of spiritual descent to any of the great Sufi orders. He is therefore generally classed as an Uvaisi Sufi, the term given to those whose spiritual initiation comes directly from divine inspiration without any saintly human intermediary.

It would however be misleading to see his poetry as the entirely original product of an unlettered genius. Shah Latif was a member of the rural elite who were trained in the Islamic sciences as transmitted through Arabic and Persian, the standard languages of education, and who themselves often wrote in these languages rather than in their native Sindhi. His great-great-grandfather Shah Abdul Karim (d. 1623) of Bulri in southern Sindh, who had been a noted spiritual teacher in his own right, also composed pioneering Sufi poems in Sindhi.[2] These were recorded soon after Karim's death in a lengthy Persian memoir composed by a disciple and are known to have been treasured by Shah Latif. He is also known to have been in contact with another *pīr* nearer to his own time, his older contemporary Shah Inat Rizvi (d. 1711) of Nasarpur, who was the author of a longer collection of Sindhi poetry strikingly similar in scope to the far more famous *Risālo.*[3] There was, therefore, already an established culture in Sindh of vernacular Sufi poetry, although this tends to be overshadowed by Shah Latif's unique reputation in the literary histories.[4]

The wide-ranging references in *Risālo* to many different locations in and around Sindh support the claim that Shah Latif traveled extensively as a young man. Like those of so many religious teachers in premodern South Asia, Shah Latif's verses were first extemporized orally in speech or song, then unsystematically recorded in writing by disciples. The *Risālo* emerged gradually from various collections of the verses Shah Latif had produced on many different occasions.

Shah Latif's growing reputation came to attract an increasing number of disciples, and he later settled in the desert near Hyderabad in lower Sindh at Bhit, a place now known in his honor as Bhitshah ("Shah's Dune"). This is the site of the magnificent tomb constructed in his honor by the local ruler Ghulam Shah Kalhoro, where the date of his death is recorded as 14 Safar a.h. 1166 (1752 CE). Although he left no son to assume responsibility for the Bhitshah shrine, his disciples ensured that it became the center of his cult, including the elaborate tradition of musical performance of his poetry that he himself had devised, and the collection of poetry by Shah Latif and others that was carefully assembled in the historic manuscript known as the *Ganj*, dated a.h. 1207 (1792 CE).

The Context

Sufi poetry is hardly to be properly appreciated without wider reference to the larger religious and literary traditions by which it is so intimately informed. In spite of the universalizing spiritual tone that is such an attractive feature of much Sufi poetry, not least in the magnificent case of the

Risālo, this first means understanding that Sufism in India is no exception to the general rule that Sufism is and always has been an integral part of Islam.[5] Although the Sufis' emphasis on the primacy of a spiritual understanding distinguished them from the legalistic constructions of the orthodox scholars, they equally found their core inspiration in the message of the Qur'an and the example of the prophet Muhammad as recorded in the Traditions known as Hadith.

Since Islam is one of the defining cases of a religion of the book, the various traditions derived from the Qur'an within Islam have each generated their own extensive bodies of literature. By the ninth and tenth centuries, Sufis were already well established in Baghdad and other cities of the Middle East. These early Sufis, like the famous martyr Mansur al-Hallaj (d. 922), naturally used Arabic as the medium for their poetry and their prose treatises. Somewhat later, when various Muslim kingdoms established an independent existence in Iran and Afghanistan, Persian came to be cultivated as a literary language written in the Arabic script and containing large numbers of Arabic loanwords. Persian soon supplanted Arabic, especially as the preferred medium for a vast poetic literature. The prime genre for this poetry was the ghazal, a short love lyric with a strongly marked single rhyme whose characteristic blending of divine and human love was endlessly explored by many ingenious poets over the succeeding centuries. Persian was also used to spectacular spiritual as well as literary effect by many Sufi poets, of whom the greatest was Jalal ud Din Rumi (d. 1273), the author of a huge collection of ghazals as well as the *Masnavī.*[6]

The latter is a long didactic poem generally regarded as the supreme masterwork of Persian Sufi literature and sometimes called "the Qur'an in the Persian language." It is known to have been a primary source of inspiration for Shah Latif.

The Muslim conquests of northern India extended this Persianate cultural world to Sindh, where Persian remained the dominant literary language of the Muslim elite down to the Mughal period and beyond.[7] As in other regions of South Asia, a strong Sufi presence was rapidly established across Sindh with the arrival of charismatic figures often associated with one or another of the main Sufi orders, like the Suhravardis and Qadiris.[8] Besides in the transmission of spiritual teaching within the circle of disciples formed around a *pīr*, the Sufi message was also transmitted to a wider audience through poetry sung by musicians attached to the Sufi shrines constructed around the tombs of saints.

Despite the disapproval of music in the clerical Islam upheld by the mullahs and *qazis*, the singing of mystical lyrics gained popularity with the increasing use of local languages for poetry that coincided with the decline of Mughal authority during the eighteenth century. While use of the vernacular by Sufi poets like Shah Latif and his Panjabi contemporary Bullhe Shah (d. 1758) has certainly helped to ensure their continuing popularity across religious boundaries and modern national frontiers today, it should also be remembered that they composed within a literary culture formally dominated by Persian, the language used in all the early prose accounts of Shah Latif's life.

Only with the British conquest of Sindh in 1843 did the

literary culture of the Sufi tradition come to be overlaid by the new patterns of modernity. Persian was quite rapidly replaced as the language of education, administration, and elite literature by English and by Sindhi, whose development was actively encouraged by the colonial authorities in Bombay.[9] As a classic that had always appealed to all sections of the Sindhi population, *Risālo* was pressed into service for the examinations prescribed by the new education syllabus.[10] As elsewhere in India, it was the Sindhi Hindus who were first drawn to participate most actively in the colonial system, and much of the new secondary literature in English or Sindhi prose on Shah Latif's life and poetry was the work of Hindu scholars.[11]

This situation continued until after independence in 1947, when the mass emigration of the Hindu population from Pakistan to India took place. Since then, studies by Indian scholars of Sindhi literature in general and of Shah Latif in particular have continued to occupy a prominent place.[12] These naturally tend to view Shah Latif as one of the many great premodern poet saints who helped to construct the national identity of modern India, and to detect the particular inspiration of the Vedanta in his exposition of universal spiritual truths. The very large literature on Shah Latif that has been produced in Pakistan has been mostly written in Sindhi or in Urdu and so has had rather less impact on international understanding. Many interpretations are naturally tied to local preoccupations, as when Shah Latif is too narrowly seen as an authentic spokesman of the Sindhi folk tradition or as an advocate of Sindhi nationalism.[13] A necessary corrective to this scholarship is provided by the common emphasis upon the Islamic character of Shah Latif's poetry.[14]

The Poetry: Form

Like so many collections of premodern Indian religious poetry, the *Risālo* is a set of lyrics primarily designed for musical performance. Most of these lyrics are in the traditional Sindhi form, which is commonly known by the Arabic word *bait* ("verse," plural *abyāt*). In earlier examples of Sindhi Sufi poetry, the *bait* is generally identical with the *dohā,* the premier short verse form of so much north Indian poetry.

Instead of this familiar two-line format, however, the *bait* as developed by Shah Latif more usually contains three or more lines, in which the order of one or more of the half-lines may be reversed, with the rhyme coming in the middle as in the Hindi *soraṭhā.*[15] The meter is fairly free, with a strict syllabic count not always being maintained, but the poetic structure of the half-lines is tightened by Shah Abdul Latif's systematic use of strongly marked alliteration in each half-line. While the halves of each line are tightly structured, the overall format of the *bait* as created by Shah Latif is quite free in the number of lines. It incorporates Arabic quotations that seldom conform exactly to the meter. The poet's signature is typically tied into the verse with alliteration.

Besides these densely expressed *abyāt,* Shah Latif also used the more relaxed format of the *vāī,* a close relative of the *kāfī,* the primary genre of Sufi poetry in Panjabi.[16] The *vāī* consists of a varying number of monorhymed single verses, preceded by a refrain repeated after each verse.

The Poetry: Matter

Risālo as a whole represents an ambitious recasting of the language of mystical love, long developed with such intricate sophistication in Persian Sufi poetry. While using some familiar Persian tropes, it draws upon a wide-ranging set of interlocking references to the scenery, society, and legends of Sindh to create a whole new imaginative world. Since it can be quite difficult to grasp parts of this world without having some idea of the whole, it is useful to begin with an overall summary of the contents of each of the musical modes called *sur* into which the verses of the *Risālo* are grouped, in this book presented as numbered chapters.[17]

The first three *surs* are collections of verses setting forth Sufi teachings, both directly and through images drawn from Persian and local poetry. "Kalyan" begins with a direct evocation of the oneness of the divine and praise of the special status of those who practice the mystical path to realize this:

> Whoever says with faith *He is one and has no equal* has accepted Muhammad, the cause of creation, with their heart and tongue. Exalted through following the divine command, they are never led astray to a false destination.[18]

The later verses of the *sur* use the familiar imagery of the ghazal to celebrate the cruel suffering inflicted by the beloved on all who truly seek him. Further images are developed in the lengthy "Yaman Kalyan," where the divine beloved appears first as a doctor, then as a blacksmith, while his lovers are described in the familiar Persian image of drinkers in a tavern. The core teaching of Sufism is explained with an explicit reference to the authority of Rumi:

> The multiplicity of creation is in search of God, and its origin is his beauty—this is what Rumi said. If you remove the veil from your heart, you will behold him within.[19]

A series of local images furnishes the material of the less closely linked *surs* that follow. "Khambhat" begins with a celebration of how the divine beloved's beauty eclipses that of the moon, before switching to an expression of desire to be taken to see him. If it is to get him there, the poet's camel, as elsewhere a symbol of the lower self, needs strict discipline to abandon the attractions of grazing where it will. The setting shifts from the desert to the ocean in the next two *surs.* These use the long-distance sea voyages annually undertaken by the Hindu traders of Sindh to locations like Aden, Gujarat, or Lanka as symbols of a mystical quest for the treasure of union with the beloved. In "Sirirag," the voyager is urged to observe continual vigilance to overcome the dangers of the journey, while in "Samundi" the focus is on the pain of separation suffered by the wives left behind while their husbands are absent on business:

> He has sailed away and left me completely abandoned. Ages have passed, but no one has returned. Oh wretched girl, the pain caused by the one who has departed will kill you.[20]

For many, the emotional heart of the *Risālo* is to be found in the following *surs,* which deal in different ways with heroines of local romantic legends.[21] These stories are loosely set in the pre-Mughal period when Sindh was ruled by the Muslim Rajput dynasties of Sumiros and Samos, but they are not related in detail. The emphasis is on the figure of the heroine, either as the object of poetic description or as a female persona for the poet to speak through in accordance with the usual convention of Indian lyric poetry.

The long "Suhini" is based upon a Sindhi story centered on the river Indus. Suhini, who has been married off to another man, uses an earthen pot as a float to help her across the river for secret assignations by night with her beloved, the buffalo herder Sahar. Her sister-in-law discovers her secret and substitutes an unfired pot, which causes Suhini to drown.

As in many other passages in the *Risālo,* the intensity of feeling provoked by the heroine's sufferings is heightened by a frequent shifting of the narrative voice from the poet to the female persona's direct speech and back again:

> Suhini was happy when she saw the designs drawn by the potter. The water washed away the pattern and the glaze could not withstand the impact. In her thoughtless youthful pride, Suhini thought it was fully fired. In the Indus she came to know that it was unbaked.
>
> "So what if it is unfired? The favor of my beloved is firm. Sahar is my beloved, it is wrong for me to look at Dam. Whether squalls or strong winds blow, I will go on to the far bank."

> The unfired pot was quite unable to withstand
> the river and it crumbled into pieces. She lost
> her strength in the stream, her arms became
> exhausted. Pouring in from all sides, the waves
> buried her. Her heart was filled with the reality of
> the angel of death.[22]

The allegorical significance of Suhini's perilous journey across the river in search of her beloved is dwelled upon at length, with numerous extended descriptions of the perils the intrepid searcher must face.

Suhini, who met her death in the river, forms a natural pair with Sasui, the delicately reared girl from the southern Sindhi city of Bhambhor, whose beloved, the Baloch prince Punhun, was abducted from her side by his kinsmen while she slept. She suffers prolonged torment from the heat and the desert as she tracks him across Las Bela to the west of Sindh, before she finally meets her end in the wilderness:

> She climbs the mountain with feet softer than silk.
> The soles of the poor girl's feet are wounded and
> gashed. Such is the sad state in which she makes
> her way toward Punhun, saying, "Oh, may he
> come back, the one to whom this slave girl is
> bound."[23]

As the greatest of all the heroines, Sasui has no fewer than five *surs* devoted to her: "Sasui Abiri," "Ma'zuri," "Desi," "Kohiyari," and "Husaini." Throughout them all, she represents the devoted lover who is determinedly set on the mystical quest for the divine beloved, of whom Punhun is the supreme symbol.

While both Suhini and Sasui are perfect incarnations of the selfless fidelity that must be displayed by the true seeker, the next two *surs* reflect the contrary fate awaiting those who do not remain true to their love in spite of their high birth. In "Lila Chanesar," Lila is fatally tempted by the offer of a valuable necklace to allow her rival Kaunru to spend the night with her royal husband, Chanesar. When he finds out how he has been shamefully deceived, he is enraged with Lila, who bitterly laments the loss of his love and of her royal status for the paltry reward of worldly riches:

> "The glitter of the gems turned my head. I thought I would win the necklace as a bet, and that it would be mine forever. Kaunru's trickery beat me."[24]

In "Mumal Rano" the enchantress Mumal, who has used sorcery to destroy all the suitors who were lured to her magic palace of Kak, is finally won by the Rajput prince Mendhiro, called Rano. But when a trick of hers goes wrong, he abandons her in jealous rage, and she is left to lament her fate and pines for him in despair.

The next two *surs* are different again. The long "Marui" is based on the story of a beautiful girl belonging to the Maru tribe of desert nomads who was abducted by the ruler Umar. Held in luxurious confinement in his fortress at Umarkot in eastern Sindh, Marui bemoans the loss of her old freedom and the absence of her beloved fellow tribesman:

> "If I die thinking about the homeland I long for, do not imprison my body in captivity. Do not keep this exile apart from her beloved. Pour the cool earth of the desert over her dead body. Once my life is over, take my corpse to Malir."[25]

In "Kamod," by contrast, there is a happy ending when the fisher girl Nuri from the Kinjhar lake in lower Sindh is overcome by gratitude for the favor shown her by Prince Tamachi, when he makes her his principal queen. Another local folktale forms the basis of the very short "Ghatu," which celebrates the heroism of a family of fishermen who battle a sea monster living in a whirlpool near Karachi.

The next three *surs* are devoted to one of most remarkable themes in the *Risālo,* the wandering yogis who traversed Sindh during their pilgrimage to the shrine of the goddess at Hinglaj in Balochistan. As a young man, Shah Latif is believed to have spent time with these yogis, whose extraordinarily single-minded focus on their spiritual quest is praised at length in the very long "Ramakali:"

> The fire of love blazes within them, while on the outside they are covered with ashes like stokers. Choosing a retreat, they have abandoned lies, vices, and falseness. They have nothing to do with sin, but practice many virtues. The more they burn, the purer and the happier they become.[26]

The celebration of the ascetic way of life of the Hindu yogis, a most unusual topic for a Sufi poet, is continued in "Khahori." After an appeal to the crow, the traditional go-between of Indian love poetry who conveys messages to the beloved, the second part of "Purab" laments the sudden departure of the yogis for their home country in the east. Another traditional bird symbol is invoked in "Karayal," which speaks of the wild goose (sometimes translated as "swan") that stands for the spiritually evolved man, as opposed to the snakes of this world described in the second part of the *sur*.

The season of the rains, always infused with intense feeling in the Indian poetic imagination, is wonderfully evoked in "Sarang," where the transformation of the landscape in Sindh and far beyond is interpreted as a manifestation of the universal extent of divine grace:

> It has rained in the plains and deserts, it has rained in Jaisalmer. The sky is overcast and the rains have come to the desert. Women left on their own have lost their worries, says Latif. The paths have been made fragrant, and the herdsmen's wives are happy.[27]

Other traditional poetic themes appear in the next three short *surs*. The sufferings of a woman whose husband has gone away are described in "Rip," while "Barvo Sindhi" is an expression of love, again through the usual female persona. "Kapaiti" explores the familiar Sufi theme of a woman spinning as a symbol of life put to productive use.

Then are *surs* variously based upon male characters from the heroic Rajput period of Sindhi history. Their generous chivalry evokes the supreme qualities of the central figure of

Muslim devotion, the prophet Muhammad. The famously munificent Sapar Khan of Las Bela is evoked as a symbol of perfect beneficence in "Piribhati." In "Sorath," the generosity of Rai Diyach of Junagarh in Gujarat is so great that he has no hesitation in allowing his head to be cut off when the minstrel Bijal asks for it as a reward for his performance.

The notably varied "Dahar" begins with an evocation of the former prosperity of an area now made desolate by the shifting course of the Indus, the grace of the Prophet, then the sorrowful cry of the lone crane abandoned by its migrating flock, before concluding with references to the brave bandit Lakho. Further praise of the prophet Muhammad as the ideal ruler begins "Bilaval," which goes on to celebrate the legendary generosity and chivalry of the Sindhi ruler Jadam Jakhiro, ending with an unusually satirical conclusion in which the poet's disciple Vagand is mocked for his laziness and greed.

The final "Kedaro" is rather different in character from the rest of *Risālo.* It too is a celebration of heroic courage, but the setting is far from Sindh in the desert of Iraq, where Imam Husain was killed at the battle of Karbala in 680. The clear alignment of this *sur* with the world of Shia mythology has raised questions about its authenticity, which is however generally maintained with some qualification.[28]

The Poetry: Manner

In considering the questions that surround this unusual *sur* "Kedaro," there is an interesting anecdote. When Shah Latif was asked if he was Sunni or Shia, he first replied that he was in between the two, and when told there was nothing in between, he gave the perfect Sufi response by stating, "I am that nothing."[29] It is, after all, this negation of the separate existence of the self that makes possible the *Risālo's* extended celebration of the wonderfully varied ways the divine is made manifest.

This ambiguity may be the fundamental reason why—in contrast to the relative ease with which the formal structures of Shah Latif's poetry, even the capacious matter of its content, may be defined—it is so much harder to pin down the distinctive manner of its expression, especially in comparison with the more familiar outspoken style of other well-known Sufi poets of the region, like his Panjabi contemporary Bullhe Shah. Shah Latif proclaims the same truth as other more outspoken Sufis while disclaiming the need always to speak of it so openly:

> The multiplicity of creation is in search of God,
> and its origin is his beauty—this is what Rumi
> believed. Those who have seen this place do not
> speak of it.[30]

Instead of reiterating the simpler kind of Sufi vision, Shah Latif in his Sindhi poetry creates for his audience an entirely new way of imagining reality. All the sources agree that he kept three books with him as his primary sources of continual inspiration: the Qur'an, from whose verses he so frequently quotes in Arabic; Rumi's great Persian *Masnavī;* and the Sindhi verses of his ancestor Shah Karim. He derived from them a genuinely new creation in his *Risālo,* in which a large collection of individual verses embracing a vast variety of local and Islamic references collectively constitute one of those all-embracing classics that most literatures are only given once. As he himself says of his poetry:

> What you consider to be poems are divine verses.
> They direct the mind toward the beloved.[31]

Here the contrast between *baita,* the ordinary Sindhi word for poems, and *āyatūn̲,* the Arabic word for verses of the Qur'an, might be seen as an indirect claim for the status of the *Risālo* as a "Qur'an in the Sindhi language" comparable to the classic definition of the *Masnavī* as a "Qur'an in the Persian language." Equally, it might well be said the *Risālo* is one of those very rare instances in the literary history of South Asia of a genuinely integral Indo-Islamic creation.[32]

The Translation

The present translation has been designed to be in keeping with the style of the Murty Classical Library of India. It tries to convey some sense of the poetry in a consistent style of plain English prose that aims to steer a middle path between off-putting formality and jarring colloquialism. While it makes no attempt to imitate the rhyme schemes of the Sindhi text, it does allow for some imitation of the alliteration that is so prominent a feature of the original, but only where this occurred naturally. So far as possible, the underlying syntax of the verses has been maintained, with a full stop marking the end of an individual line and a comma being used where appropriate to indicate the half-line caesura. Italics are used to mark Shah Latif's quite frequent citation of Qur'anic verses and other Arabic and Persian quotations.[33]

Since throughout the *Risālo* the lyrical immediacy of individual verses is always more prominent than any regular narrative or didactic progression, the first endnote to each *sur* provides an overview of its contents. It is therefore recommended that these initial endnotes be consulted before reading each chapter.

NOTES

1 The two best studies in English are Sorley 1966 and Schimmel 1976. See also Advani 1970, Baloch 1972, Jhangiani 1987, Lalwani 1978, Mirza 1980, Sayed 1988.

2 Jotwani 1996 includes a complete translation of Shah Karim's Sindhi verses.

3 A small selection is translated in Allana 1996. But the findings of the excellent pioneering edition by Baloch (1963) have yet to be reflected in the English critical literature.

4 For the history of early Sindhi poetry, see further Ajwani 1970, Schimmel 1974. Asani 2003 is particularly good on the different traditions of this poetry.

5 For an informed introduction to Sufism, see Ernst 1997.

6 Schimmel 1982 remains the best introduction to Sufi poetry in Persian and other languages.

7 Sadarangani 1987 is an excellent source for the now forgotten Persian poetry written by the educated elite in the Mughal capital of Thatta and other urban centers in Sindh.

8 Boivin 2015 is a most helpful guide to the history of the Sufi culture of Sindh. Rizvi 1978–1983 is the standard general account of the Sufi orders in India. For their distribution in Sindh, see Ansari 1992: 9–35.

9 Because Sindh was administered from Bombay rather than Calcutta, Urdu was not installed as the immediate successor of Persian, as happened in Panjab.

10 Compare Richard Burton's notice of Shah Latif in his classic firsthand account of premodern Sindh (Burton 1851: 81–84).

11 See further the pioneering study of Shah Latif in English by Lalwani 1978, besides the major early edition of the *Risālo* by Gurbakhshani [1923–1931] 1979.

12 Compare Ajwani 1970; Jotwani 1975, 1996.

13 See for example Syed 1996.

14 In English, this has been cogently argued by Schimmel, whose work remains an essential introduction to Shah Latif and his *Risālo*. Schimmel 1976.

15 Lines in this reversed order of the *sorațhā* are most commonly found in the concluding verse of *abyāt* and in the opening refrain of a *vāī*, as illustrated in the following examples, but are by no means confined to these positions.

16 Compare the Bullhe Shah *kāfī* transliterated in Shackle 2015: xvi–xvii.

17 More detailed guides will be found in the introductory endnote to each chapter.

18 Verse 1.2.

19 Verse 2.71.

20 Verse 6.7.

21 These are often collectively referred to as "the seven heroines" (S. *sat sūrmiyūṉ*), viz. Suhini, Sasui, Lila, Mumal, Marui, Nuri, and Sorath; see further Sayed 1988 and Hussain 2001. "Sorath" hardly deals with the princess after whom the *sur* is named, and is accordingly placed separately in our numerical sequence.

22 Verses 7.90-7.92.

23 Verse 8.56.

24 Verse 13.5.

25 Verse 15.44.

26 Verse 18.52.

27 Verse 22.14.

28 It is omitted without comment in Kazi 1961. In Baloch 2012: 417–425 it is placed separately, immediately following the main body of *surs* now generally agreed to be fully authentic, and preceding a variety of extra *surs* that were present in earlier editions. These notably include a certainly inauthentic Hir and a Dhol Marui that extend the geographical coverage of the *Risālo* to Panjab and to Rajasthan.

29 Advani 1970: 32.

30 Verse 2.71.

31 Verse 7.77.

32 In this sense, the *Risālo* might be seen as an achievement in lyric poetry fully comparable to the narrative poetry of the earlier Avadhi *premākhyān,* now better known since Behl 2012.

33 The translations of Qur'anic verses are based on Yusuf Ali 1977.

THE RISALO OF SHAH ABDUL LATIF

1 Kalyan

First there is Allah, the all-knowing, the highest, the lord of the world. All-powerful through his own power, he is everlasting and immemorial. Lord unique, *he is one,*[1] the provider and merciful lord. Magnify the true lord, and utter praise of the one who is all-wise. It is he who in his mercy ensures all the workings of the universe. 1

Whoever says with faith *He is one and has no equal*[2] has accepted Muhammad, the cause of creation, with their heart and tongue. Exalted through following the divine command, they are never led astray to a false destination. 2

Never led astray to a false destination, they reach their goal safely. Possessing mystic wisdom, they are united as one with the one God. From the outset, the master has made them priceless and happy. 3

From the outset, the master has made them pure light. *There is no fear upon them, nor are they sorrowful.*[3] They are true and have no pain. The lord has caused their fortunes to flourish from the beginning of eternity. 4

Smitten by *he is one,* they recite *except God.*[4] With hearts joined to truth, they traverse the way. 5

In the silent wonder of gnosis, they search the mystical realm.[5] They never sleep at ease, nor do they spend their time sitting around. Lovers cut their heads from their shoulders, says Abdul Latif.

6 Are you deaf? Have you not heard that *He is one and has no equal?* Why have your ears not heard the galloping steeds within your heart? You will shed bitter tears when the witnesses[6] appear before you.

7 *He is one and has no equal* is the profitable practice that you should follow. This world, where you win or lose, is your place. It is the beloved who will fill the cup of paradise and who will tell you to drink.

8 The key to unity is that *He is one and has no equal.* Those who have embraced duality are lost.

9 I look for my head and do not find my body. I look for my body and there is no head. Where have my severed hands, wrists, and fingers gone? If they went in union with oneness, they have been permanently cut off.

10 Do not call him "lover," and do not call him "beloved." Do not call him "creator," you fool, do not call him "created." Reveal the mystic secret to the one who has been freed from imperfection.

From unity came multiplicity, the total of multiplicity 11
is unity. Reality is indeed one; do not be misled by
speaking in any other way. I swear to God that this
whole tumult is created by the beloved.

It is he who is *great is his glory,*[7] and he who is the 12
soul of beauty. It is he who is the form of the
beloved, and he who is perfect beauty. It is he who
becomes the master and the disciple, and it is he
who is himself the original idea.[8] This entire state
becomes known from within.

It is he who looks at himself, it is he who is his beloved. 13
It is he who creates the beauties of the universe, it
is he who desires them.

The echo is the utterance, if you understand the 14
mystery of speech. They were originally together,
but became two in the hearing.

There is one palace, with thousands of doors, and 15
it has millions of windows. The master appears
before me wherever I look.

You have thousands, hundreds of thousands, or 16
millions of forms. Creatures all seem quite
separate from one another. Oh my beloved, how
can I describe all your signs?

Everyone worships the beloved. 17V
It is the quality of love that it is created by the eyes.

The beloved knows everything I think of in my mind.
The sound of Latif's sweet song finds a hearing.

18 My sickness pleased my beloved and his heart was touched. I experienced true health after mounting the scaffold.

19 Why do you hurt me so, you blind and stupid doctor? My body is racked by pain, but you just give me doses of medicine. Those who make the scaffold their bed find that death grants them the vision of their beloved.

20 The scaffold has always been a proud adornment for lovers. They stand there openly, considering it a disgrace to retreat or turn aside. Lovers have always promised to be slain.

21 What accounts for lovers rejoicing on the scaffold? Once they exchanged glances with the beloved, the scaffold became their marriage bed.

22 You may have to mount the scaffold a hundred times a day, but do not become discouraged and abandon the idea of love. The secret of love is revealed only when you have seen its other side.

23 First put the knife on your throat, then ask about love. Play on the suffering inflicted by the beloved on

the body like an instrument. If you have sworn by the name of love, let your flesh be roasted on spits.

It is not the fault of the knife, it is the one who holds 24
the handle who slays me. The iron trembles at the sight of the wonderful ways of the beloved. Lovers always pine for those whom they love.

May his knife not be sharp, let it rather be blunt. That 25
will cause the hands of my beloved to linger over me.

Those in front are on the execution blocks, while those 26
who follow have their heads prepared. To avoid being thought less than them, cut off your own head and gain acceptance. Do you not see the heads of the slain lying on the ground? Slaughter rages in the distiller's shop.

If you yearn for a drink, go to the distiller's still. 27
Remove your head, says Latif, and place it by the wine jar. Bridegroom, drink a mouthful of this strong wine. At the price of a head, the wine that intoxicates young heroes comes cheap.

If you yearn for a drink, go to the street of the 28
distillers. There you will always find the divine wine of Shiv.[9] When I worked out the riddle, it was that the wine is a good bargain in exchange for a head.

29 You cannot get the wine for cash; it is more valuable than that. Prepare to get your head cut off, says Shah. This is the place of those who die beside the wine jars.

30 Lovers are drinkers of poison, and they are delighted when they see it. They are ever accustomed to its bitter and deadly taste. They have been smitten by love, says Latif, and have been destroyed by separation. Even though their wounds fester, they do not even sigh in public.

31 Do not desire the wine if you want to avoid its bitter taste. The soul of those who have drunk it leaves their veins. Enjoy the jar of wine, says Latif, once you have removed your head.

32 Why do those who falsely desire it keep talking about wine? They turn back once the distillers draw their blades. It is those who give their heads in exchange for it who get to drink draughts of the wine.

33 Their heads are separated from their bodies, chunks of their flesh cook in the pot. Ready with their heads in their hands, they can talk about the wine.

34 It is not the first task of lovers to preserve their heads. A moment with their beloved is far better than a

hundred heads. This skin and bones cannot match a taste of the beloved.

Everyone would long to offer their heads, if in 35
exchange they could be with him. If the deal was done by sacrificing their heads, lovers would freely come. If it is written in their fate, they find their precious beloved.

A drop of that wine is very precious, and the price of 36
desire is martyrdom. Our task is to worship; the beloved's role is to cast his glance of grace.

As I drank the wine, I recognized the beloved 37V
properly;
Drinking the cup of love, we understood everything.
Awareness of the beloved is like a fire within us.
Life in this world lasts for a couple of days at most.
Oh God, says Abdul Latif, you are all that there is.

After arousing pain inside me, the beloved has 38
departed. He has gone after inflicting suffering. The doctors' talk is utterly displeasing to me now.

Those who take the beloved for their guide suffer 39
a severe illness. The doctor does not make the slightest difference to them. The beloved shows the way, and he is the medicine that restores them to health.

40 The beloved is the medicine that restores them to health, he is not the suffering. In company he seems sweet, but when summoned he is full of wrath. He uses his dagger to stab those to whom he shows his friendship. The master, lord, and forgiver of faults causes life to circulate through the veins.

41 My veins have become an instrument that plays all the time. The lover cannot speak but can only writhe about when the beloved provides no response. It is the lover who bandages the one he has killed. It is he who is pure torment, he who is comfort for the soul.

42 It is he who bars the way, he who is the guide. *You exalt whom you will and you bring low whom you will.*[10]

43 Why do you long to be greeted, why not offer greeting yourself? Other doors are forbidden to those who have seen this door.

44 Sweeter than sweetness, his words are not at all bitter. From the beloved, silence is a greeting.

45 Nothing but sweetness comes from the beloved. If you taste it carefully, there is no bitterness.

46 The one you think of thinks of you too. You need to understand the verse *Remember me and I will*

remember you.[11] He has a knife in his hand and sugar in his mouth—this is the way he shows he cares.

The beloved once asked me with a smile, *Am I not your* 47
lord?[12] Ever since he said that, the sharp pain I felt has not left me.

They smile and ask, “Where is the beloved’s hand?” 48
When pinned down by the spear of love, they do not turn aside. Lovers come before death with their necks unbowed. Those for whom being slain is intimacy experience death as the revelation of the beloved.

The beloved kills through calling, and calls through 49
killing. When pinned down by the spear of love, do not turn aside. Oh lover, destroy your awareness and advance toward death.

Calling lovers is the same as driving them away. This 50
paradox is the essence of love’s response. Never give up hope, for their separation is their joining.

When he kills he cares, when he cares he kills. He is 51
the one who destroys, mother, and he is the one who is the soul’s comfort.

When he kills he cares; it is the beloved who calls. 52
This is the unvarying habit that he has learned.

The one who wounds is the doctor, and the soul's
comfort.

53V The beloved will be my body's doctor, and the cure for
my pain.
He will give me a dose of his mercy. Oh, may the
beloved come.
The beloved has come himself to take care of this poor
patient.
The doctor has removed all pain from my body.
Oh sisters, says Abdul Latif, the beloved is a skilled
physician.

2 *Yaman Kalyan*

You are the beloved, you are the doctor, and you are 1
the remedy for pain. Beloved, my heart holds hurts of many kinds. Lord, grant healing to this sick patient.

You are the beloved, you are the doctor, and you are 2
the medicine for pain. You give pain to those who suffer, oh generous one, and you remove their pain from them. Powders make a difference when you issue your instructions.

Take aim, beloved, and let your arrow fly and strike 3
me. Let this be the occasion for me to seek refuge on your lap, and in this way let me come close to you.

When the beloved fires his arrows filled with love, 4
doctors forget their expertise.

Beloved, if you are merciful and strike me, I will not 5
consult a doctor but will live with my wounds.

The arrow-struck groan from the pain of the steel tips 6
that pierce their limbs. Steeped in passion, they writhe on the battlefield of love. They bandage and treat their wounds themselves. Oh, come and spend a night with those who are wounded.

7 Come and spend a night with those who are wounded, whose bodies are filled with pain and whose hearts are smitten. Hiding away from people, they bandage their wounds themselves.

8 Today the wounded keep groaning in their huts. When evening falls, they put those same bandages and plasters on their wounds.

9 Those who are fit have no awareness of pain, or of how the wounded exist. Lying on the floor, the wounded cannot turn from side to side. Alas, they are tormented in secret for the beloved and shed tears. Those who truly think of him spend the whole night weeping.

10 Those who are fit have no awareness of pain, while the sick are groaning. They lie on the floor, gripped by serious illness. They are filled with love, says Latif, and they are in permanent pain. Those whose love is perfect spend the whole night weeping.

11 Mother, I do not believe those who shed tears and show people how their eyes water. Those who truly think of the beloved do not weep or say anything.

12 Doctor, you know nothing about the pain my body suffers. Gather up your medicines, dig a hole, and bury them in the ground. I have no need of life without my beloved.

They argue with their doctors and do not follow the 13
treatment they prescribe. If they followed their
advice, they would quickly become well.

Doctors have great compassion for the sick. They do 14
their best for them, but nothing happens unless
their instructions are followed.

When doctors were my neighbors I never consulted 15
them, because there were cataracts in my eyes.

You fool, you became lax in your diet and harmed 16
your body. If you had followed the prescribed
treatment, you would have regained your
strength.

If you think of being united with the beloved, then 17
learn from the way that thieves behave. They
celebrate by keeping awake and taking no rest all
night long. When they deliberately do come out,
they do not utter a word. When they are chained
together and put on the gallows, they say nothing.
Although they are cut with knives, they reveal
nothing of what has really happened.

The doctors threaten the wounded ones and drive 18
them away from their house. Their wounds break
open and fester, forming no scabs. Their wounds
are relieved by seeing the beloved. Once the
doctors depart in disgust, oh my beloved, may I
arise refreshed.

19 It is the one who inflicted my wounds who became my doctor. He quickly tied my bandages and made me better in a day. Stay with him, oh my heart, so that you may not be wounded.

20 Do not give me medicine, doctor, in case I get well. Perhaps my beloved will come sometime to ask after me.

21 You were with the doctors, so how did you become weak? Why did you not give your head, and get medicines in exchange for it?

22 Bad doctors cut me and did not put me together. The ignorant branded me, and gave my body pain.

23 The patients paid no attention at all to the doctors' treatment. They were far from the medicines that the doctors talked about.

24 The doctors tried their various medicines and treatments on me. He checks my pulse and gives me the medicine of his mercy. Pain is removed from those who are treated by the beloved.

25 The sick gathered today and appealed for health. Be off with you, pain, the merciful one has shown his face.

26 "Alas, alas!" is my heart's lament for my beloved. My liver and my kidneys are roasted in the fire of love.

If you do not believe me, look at the flames that burn above me.

Let me roast on burning sticks of thorn and acacia, with my liver, heart, and kidneys, all three of them on skewers. Now beyond the doctors' care, I am in the power of the beloved. 27

The arrow my beloved aimed and fired a second time quickly hummed and whistled as it came. It cut through my liver, heart, and kidneys. It has become so stuck inside my body that it will not come out, however hard I pull. 28

Ask the moths what burning is like. They hurl themselves into the fire, and their hearts are pierced by the lances of love. 29

If you call yourself a moth, come and extinguish the fire. The fire has burned many people; now put it out. Become aware and extinguish it; do not give the fire to ordinary people. 30

If you call yourself a moth, do not turn away when you see the fire. Enter the beloved's brightness and become his bridegroom. You are still unbaked and have no experience of the furnace. 31

The moths made a plan and collected over the fire. 32
The sight of the scorching heat did not make them

tremble, and they were burned in the fire of truth. Many of the poor creatures were consumed.

33 If your body burns like a furnace, cool it down with a sprinkling of patience. Light the fire of discipline and burn your being. Complete all the stages of your spiritual journey in secrecy. Never reveal your passion, says Latif. Otherwise people may find out, and an obstacle may be created in the way of your union.

34 It was only yesterday that the beloved took me out of the oven. Then he increased the heat to get me to union faster. For lovers the fire never grows less.

35 They heat ore and produce steel. Only expert blacksmiths know about them.

36 Today too the blacksmiths' strokes clang loudly. They heat the fire of love, heaping on the coals. Stoker, do not back away, in case the unsmelted steel breaks into pieces.

37 Stoker, do not stoke the fire, and do not go near it. You cannot bear the flames of love, although you stand there and proclaim yourself to be a blacksmith.

38 Make your head an anvil, then ask for the blacksmith. Under his blows, you may become one with the steel.

Like the anvil, suffer blow upon blow. Let yourself be 39
harshly beaten, and obliterate yourself in love.

Today the blacksmiths have come, experts with the 40
whetstone. They whet it with water to sharpen
swords.

Today the blacksmiths have come, expert and able. 41
They will remove the rust and reveal the steel.

I have seen the happiness of those who know how to 42
use the whetstone. Their swords are never stained
with rust.

One cup and two people—this is not how love works. 43
How will counting get anyone near the beloved?
See how their sense of separate existence has
deprived them of union.

One cup and two people—this is not how love works. 44
Those who are held fast in love's embrace dissolve
and become one. The dagger of closeness cuts
duality in two.

One cup and two people—love does not share things 45
out. Oh poet, you have acquired this desire from
the singer.[1]

Slayers of the self have learned how to turn poison 46
into honey. Sit with them and drink a few cups.

47 Never hide what you have from drinkers. Give the travelers who walk past plenty to drink. Oh wine seller, that will make your shop popular.

48 Never hide what you have from drinkers. Give the travelers a cup to drink, and see how they will give lakhs for every drop you give them.

49 The drinkers choke as they drink from cups of poisoned wine. "*Cupbearer, arise and give us wine.*[2] Let your friends drink," they say. They are not satisfied with sips, but secretly eye the full jars of wine.

50 The wind blows from the north, the wine seller has opened his jars. The drinkers have prepared their heads for the taste.

51 Sprinkle the dew of the tavern on the travelers. Everyone will know about it and its praises will be sung everywhere, when the morning drinkers have come into your courtyard.

52 When they come into your courtyard, they polish off the wine. Their thirst remains the same; after one drink they call for another.

53 The wine seller is no gentleman, but comes from a low caste. He destroys the drinkers by pouring cups of wine down their throats.

The drinkers are dead. Oh wine seller, don't you die. 54
Oh sufferer, how will you manage without your
generous supplier?

The drinkers have died. You too should die, wine 55
seller. Who besides them will endure your
threatening behavior?

They were not killed by the wine, but by what the 56
wine seller said. It was the distiller's words that
wounded their hearts. Afterward death came to
the drinkers.

To have a dagger at their throats and a cup at their lips 57
is the drinkers' way. They take large draughts and
are overcome. Those who attain ecstasy drink a
lot of wine.

The wine seller did not wish them ill, nor did he kill 58
them with poison. They gathered there for a
drink, says Shah. Those who were overcome by
what he said lie buried beside his stills.

Give your head and somehow make a deal with the 59
distiller. Stab your skull with a knife, a saw, or a
dagger. Do not turn away from death; a cup costs
more than that.

There is something new in every cup, a different wine 60
in every jar. Drinkers know the distiller's delight.

They come right into his shop, ready to sacrifice their heads. To drink a drop they happily they give their heads, says Shah.

61 Oh my heart, why did you not learn from the distillers? Their nights are spent in weeping and in drawing liquor from their stills.

62 Those Sufis who left multiplicity aside went safely. Those who play the game of love never forget it. In consultation with the beloved, they reached their goal through drunkenness.

63 The Sufi travels through everything, like breath through the veins. He does not say anything about the closing formula.[3] For him it is a sin to reveal this.

64 They are grieved by being given, by not being given they are happy. True Sufis are those who take nonexistence with them.

65 *The Sufi is no Kufi,*[4] no one understands him. His struggle takes place within, leaving no external mark. He is on the side of those who are at odds with him.

66 The Sufi has washed clean the page of his existence. Afterward, while still alive, he gets to see the beloved.

It is unfitting for a Sufi to call himself one and yet to be 67
full of desire. Cut up your tall Sufi cap and throw
it into the fire.

If you wear a Sufi cap, then be a proper Sufi. Take a 68
cup of poison in your hand and drink it all up.
This is the place of those who have attained
ecstasy.

Pitch the secret tent of almighty God in your body.[5] 69
Recite the spoken formula all day long. Carefully
seek out his holy name in the Qur'an. Do not
search at other doors; it is here that this precious
treasure is found.

Full of ego, the world wanders lost, not realizing that 70
this magic show is created by the divine magician.

The multiplicity of creation is in search of God, and its 71
origin is his beauty—this is what Rumi believed.[6]
Those who have seen this place do not speak of it.

The multiplicity of creation is in search of God, and its 72
origin is his beauty—this is what Rumi believed.
Where did man come from to be here? Do you not
see the magic that has been performed?

The multiplicity of creation is in search of God, and its 73
origin is his beauty—this is what Rumi said. If you
remove the veil from your heart, you will behold
him within.

74 On the outside they are fornicators, but they are lost in contemplation. The arrow of true teaching has pierced their inner being. They recite the holy name of God in their hearts.

75 Those who have learned the formula of pain, recite the lesson of suffering. Holding the slate of contemplation, they study in silence. They recite from the page on which they see the beloved.

76 They do not remember the line that begins with *alif.*[7] Uselessly they look for the beloved on other pages.

77 They remember the line that begins with *alif. There is no other purpose in both worlds* [*besides God*] [8]—this is what he said. Discovering the narrow path, they found delight in God the merciful.

78 Why did you study letters, you wretch, and become a *qazi?* Do not approach here in delusion and conceit. Ask Azazil[9] about the taste of this drink.

79 Azazil is the true lover; the others are all full of empty desire. He became accursed because of his abundant love.[10]

80 When I studied the lesson of the beginning[11] for myself, I first discovered my own abode, the place

where the souls are daily engaged in gnosis. The page was turned and the breach in my union with the divine was healed.[12]

The learned keep reading but do not suffer in their hearts. The faster they turn the pages, the higher their sins mount up. 81

Read the letter *alif,* forget all the other pages. Light up your inner self; how many pages will you read? 82

As you turn the pages, the more sins you see. What use is talking about him if the beloved is not present? 83

Oh scribe, just as you write *lām* joined to *alif,*[13] so does the beloved remain joined to our soul. 84

A forty-day vigil[14] is not equal to a sight of the beloved. Oh scribe, why do you pile pages on pages? You may turn twenty pages, but the letter[15] is the same. 85

The body is a mosque and the mind is a cell; do not keep a forty-day vigil. Why do you not worship God the unseen twenty-four hours a day? Examine yourself and see him before you in everyone. The beloved is inside my mind; I was ignorant but now have realized this. 86

87 He stands before everyone. There is no place without him. What is to be done with the cowards who are separate from God the one? Only now has this ignorant creature realized that the beloved is inside my mind.

88 He is as majestic as David;[16] the beggars possess no distinction. Carelessly, he lets his armed retinue be trampled by his horse.

89 He is as majestic as David; the beggars possess no awareness. He is fully aware as he lets them be trampled by his horse.

90 Cruel as Cain,[17] you have sharp arrows in your eyes. You arise and deal violently with the intoxicated ones where they live. Beloved, such is the damage you cause with your eyes.

91 If he fits an arrow to his bow, use your chest as a shield. Experience the beloved's wounds and blows on your face. Do not doubt the gallows, but act as a true lover and be saved.

92 If he fits an arrow to his bow, use your chest as a shield. Steadfastly suffer whatever the beloved does to your face. Do not step back, but act as a true lover and be saved.

Sir, do not fit an arrow to your bow to kill me. You are inside me, so you may be hit by your own weapon. 93

False lovers escape the arrow and never let themselves be struck. Those who make themselves a mark are killed by the first shot. 94

I stand where his arrow struck me. In his mercy, perhaps my warlike beloved will strike me with another. 95

On the field of love make the earth resound. With your head on the gallows and your body on the battlements, be sure to say nothing at all. Love is without doubt a snake, as those who have been bitten know. 96

On the field of love, do not care about your head. If you mount the gallows of the beloved you will find perfect health. Love is a snake, as those who have been bitten know. 97

Love is not a game played by youths. It breaks the connection of mind, body, and soul. Put your head on the point of a spear and be cut in half. 98

God is never forgotten by his lovers. They breathe their last, sighing for him. 99

100 Lovers are not fit and well like you. Every day they go to the beloved's door and weep. In no other way can they find acceptance with him.

101 If a lover has any blood in his body, let him make no claim to love. A pale face and loss of beauty are the conditions of desire. He carries no money, but uses his head to trade with.

102 The touch of a straw still draws blood from you. How will you bear the beloved's wounds on your face? So why do you long for love?

103 Desire and death[18] both begin with the same letter. For them both to be achieved it is necessary to sit on the road that leads to the beloved, and to sacrifice one's life.

104 Either learn love, or else watch those who practice love. Do not hide with people who know nothing of love.

105 Oh lover, keep sitting in the beloved's street. Do not lose heart and quit his door. He will give you medicine of mercy that will heal your wounds. We cannot manage without you, beloved, how can you manage without us?

Oh lover, keep sitting in the beloved's shop. Bow down 106
before him with humbly covered head, so that you
may always live with him with honor.

Oh lover, keep sitting in the beloved's passageway. 107
Do not lose heart and give up the wine seller's jar.
Drink a few cups in exchange for your head.

It is foolishness to go the beloved's door all the time. 108
Do not hurry to his neighborhood, you crazy
creature. Do not be naïve and tell passersby about
it. Through suffering, says Latif, he will bring you
happiness. Share your love in secret talk between
yourselves.

Those who have suffered pain were granted health. 109
For lovers misery is sweet.

If he himself gives you water, become a camel and 110
drink it thirstily. No one previously entered this
pool without being invited.

What is unsaid does not become apparent, what is 111
said no one understands. It is true and like gold,
but does not appeal to people.

What is unsaid does not become apparent, what is 112
said no one understands. It is a golden guide to
those whom fate has favored.

113 If he breaks his ties with you, twist them together again like a thread. If he finds faults in you, you foolish wretch, consider them virtues. Go and beg him humbly to restore this beautiful connection.

114 Bow down and be patient as you search; anger will bring you grief. You will gain awareness if you stand firm in this course.

115 Be patient, for those who are patient succeed, while those who quarrel lose. Talkers do not taste the delights of forbearance.

116 There is peace in the homes of the patient, but talkers do not prosper. From having words, trouble ensues and nothing is gained.

117 If they talk against you, say nothing back to them in turn. The one who makes the first move suffers. Those who are inspired by ill will gain nothing from it.

118 Nothing is gained from ill will. If the bow is drawn too hard, the bowstring snaps.

119 Say nothing to those who do not talk against you and forget the words of those who do. Follow this practice twenty-four hours a day. With your head upon your knees, live in lowliness. Keep a

legal adviser[19] within you, so that you will not be helpless before the judge.

Oh body, settle near those who instead of snapping rudely back answer politely in different ways.[20] 120

Sitting with some people brings you much suffering. Avoid their company and gain a thousand benefits. 121

Sitting with some people brings you an absence of suffering. Oh body, settle near them and spend time there. 122

Friends, I am slain by separation from my dear beloved. 123V
At the beloved's door there are many lovers like me.
All over the place the beloved's beauty is proclaimed.
Realize that special dust trodden by his feet is perfect kohl for the eyes.
Abdul Latif says: my beloved is eternally beautiful.

3 *Asa*

1 I search for him through infinity but find no limit to the guide. The beauty of the beloved has no height or length. On this side there is incalculable longing, on that side the beloved has no concern.

2 No one ever made it across with the "I." *God is an odd number, and that is what he loves,*[1] so get rid of duality. Before unity, dissolve your existence in tears.

3 A curse on duality! Beloved, stop me from the self. Keep back the "I." May the "you" reach you, lord.

4 There is no "that" without "this,"[2] nor is "this" separate from "that." Understand the saying *Man is my secret and I am his secret.*[3] This is the refrain repeated by mystics and gnostics.

5 So long as you can see yourself, your prayer is of no use. Get rid of all your aids, and then say "God is great."

6 So long as you can see yourself, your prostration is of no use. Get rid of your existence, and then say "God is great."

Through adopting nonexistence, creatures were exalted. 7
Concealed in outward form, the real shape of the divine
was kept. What can be said here of the beloved's secret?

Those who have destroyed their existence are *effaced in* 8
God.[4] There is no standing or sitting in prayer for them,
nor do they perform prostrations. While nonexistent,
they are joined with existence.

If your eyes do not see the beloved as soon as the sun rises, 9
take them both out and feed them to the crows.

Take out your eyes before you break your fast and present 10
them to the beloved. Seeing the beloved's face is equal
to eating seventy dishes.

Eyes that have beheld the beloved at dawn have had their 11
breakfast. Entering his presence is as if one's being,
body, and soul have performed the Hajj.

At dawn the eyes come to see the beloved. Standing in 12
worship, they do nothing else. Dyed without alum, they
delight in the company of the beloved.

Every day they weep and they rejoice to see the beloved. 13
They keep coming back after seeing him, but even so
they keep searching. They never have been sated with
seeing him, nor ever will be.

14 The eyes are angry and furious with the eyes. Since they learned to long for him, the whole business makes them quarrel. They laugh and are annoyed, they are cross and they are happy with themselves.

15 I have placed many obstacles in the path of the eyes. Treading the world in their sleep, they have found the beloved. After killing me, they return satisfied with themselves.

16 The eyes take counsel between themselves. They go where life is in danger. The only thing that avails there is to sacrifice one's life.

17 The eyes fell in love without asking me. They went and got caught in the place from which there is no escape. Consumed with pain, my poor heart waits fretting beside the road to the beloved.

18 Decide to do the opposite, oh my eyes, and go the other way from most people. If people flow downstream with the current, you should flow upstream. Look straight ahead, and go back toward the beloved.

19 The beauty of the beloved is turned away. But if he turns around to face me, my veins are filled with delight and my body is filled with fresh energy.

Keep the eyes with which you can see the beloved. Do 20
not look at others, for the beloved is very jealous.

Do not look at the beloved with the physical eyes that 21
are in your face. Those eyes cannot recognize the
beloved by gazing at him. It is those who close
them who see the beloved.

Do not make these physical ones your friends, do not 22
look around with these dark eyes. You fool, why
do you not ask for the path to the true beloved?

There is plenty of guidance on the straight path, but I 23
am led astray. Seeking and getting are both near at
hand. My being is set on the place where there is
no "is" and no "is not."

Where there is no "is" and no "is not" is not something 24
that can be conceived by earthly man. The beauty
of the beloved is beyond the power of sight.

Until you make your body thinner than a needle, how 25
will the beloved find you in his eyes?

Come and dwell in my eyes, and I will close them. The 26
world will not see you, and I will not see anyone
else.

27 May some poisonous snake, some cobra come out and bite my rival, who stands there listening to the murmured words of the beloved.

28 The beloved performs straightforward actions, but in people's minds they are twisted. To understand the puzzling ways of the beloved is difficult.

29 Reason is lost in wonder, it cannot grasp anything. A blind person cannot understand the beauty of the beloved.

30 Reason collapses in wonder, it breaks into pieces. A blind person cannot understand the hints given by love.

31 The blind men quarreled about the dead elephant.[5] They felt with their hands, being unable to see with their eyes. Actually,[6] only the sighted can recognize the elephant. The power of helping us see is vested in our spiritual masters.

32 They died deprived. They did not become masters before their death. They left like sparrows pecking their way out of a pile of grass. They were just like bubbles in the valley of this world.

33 We are the same as the one we long for. Go and enter the place where *he does not beget, nor is he*

begotten.[7] From that place, oh seeker, seek out divine reality.

If you can see properly, you will say that everything is divine reality. Oh blind polytheist, do not doubt this truth. 34

Get rid of doubt, of the polytheism that gets in the way of affirming God's existence. There is nothing like the denial in which that existence is affirmed. 35

Faith does not come about by claiming to recite the profession of faith, when the heart is filled with deceit, polytheism, and the devil. That makes you a Muslim in appearance, but an Azar[8] within. 36

You are false in your unbelief, so do not call yourself an unbeliever. You are certainly no Hindu, nor are you worthy of the sacred thread. The forehead mark is properly put on those who are true to polytheism. 37

Your face is clearer than a mirror, but you are black at heart. On the outside your speech sounds fair, but in your heart you are foul. Thinking like this does not bring one near to union. 38

Apply the mascara stick of union to your eyes. Get rid of double vision, and enjoy the state of gnosis. It is wrong to find any fault with the beauty of the 39 beloved. Look with the eyes of *I bear witness*[9] so that you may be reckoned a true Muslim.

40 The blackness of mascara is suitable for women. As a man, do not apply blackness with a stick. Put the redness of the beloved on your eyes.

41 When they put red mascara on their eyes, they saw the splendor of a scarlet wedding outfit.

42 When they put white mascara on their eyes, they saw whiteness in the world.

43 I hid it thoroughly, but it was shown clearly by my tears. Suspicion was aroused in those wretches by my tears. My color was my foe, and revealed my secret.

44 Hundreds of thousands of rivers all swirl and seethe within me. May I burn inside, without any smoke escaping.

45 The self is a veil over yourself; listen and mark this well. It is existence that stands in the way of union.

46 Seeker, listen to this: the self is a veil over yourself. When there is no prevarication, all veils are removed.

"It is in me that 'I' is produced, so I am worthy of 'I.' 47
It is the awareness of 'I' that produces the 'I' from me." This applies only to him,[10] it is not for you to say.

Love is not created in a grain jar, meat is not cooked in 48
husks. How can faulty methods be used to bring about union with the beloved?

I cannot bear him looking at me closely for a second. 49
Seeing him is a distant prospect; even mentioning his name causes me distress.

My beloved tied me up and threw me into deep water. 50
He just stood there and told me not to get the hem of my clothes wet.

How can someone who falls into deep water be sure 51
of not getting wet? Oh traveler on the mystical path, teach me a method of keeping the hem of my clothes dry.

Make the Way your support, recognize the Law. Get 52
your heart used to Reality and know the place of Gnosis.[11] Remain resolute and keep safe from getting wet.

Never utter falsehood, consider it to be a dry branch. 53
Be aware, oh deserving one, and like the yogis keep your loincloth tight. That way you will make

it across while keeping all four corners of your hem dry.

54 You just sleep, demanding a comfortable bed, and do not trouble yourself at all. But unless you please the beloved, you will not be reckoned of any account.

55 They who please the beloved are the ones who will enjoy their marriage beds. Standing as *Those who believe and are constant in righteousness,*[12] they are chosen and are adorned as bridegrooms.

56 Sleep is meritorious for those who are united with the beloved. Getting their eyes used to sleep, they dream happy dreams. Waiting and pain are far from their hearts.

57 For those whose body is a rosary, whose mind is a bead, and whose heart is the lute, the strings of seeking resound with the mystery of unity. *He is one and he has no partner*[13] is the tune their veins play. They are awake even when asleep, for sleep is their worship.

58V There is something about these old huts we see.
Although no one notices those who live there, they are accepted at his door.
They are considered strangers, but they eat with the beloved.

My saints are beneath my robe[14] is the clothing in
which he dresses them.
No one besides me recognizes them.[15] He does not let
them be seen as strangers.
Leave your own ideas on the ground, and follow what
they think.
Serve them courteously, humbly covering your head.
Sisters, says Abdul Latif, it is here that you will find
something.

4 *Khambhat*

1 The beloved is goodness, because he is goodness. In his mercy he does not confront me or offer reproaches. I am surrounded by defects, but the beloved is filled with good qualities.

2 Oh moon, you are the one who sees my beloved there. Give him the message I give you as I weep. May I be together with him, and may he not go away.

3 May my beloved be together with me, and may he have no occasion to go away, he whose eyes dwell in my soul. My heart relies on his support, he whose words are measured.

4 The night is bright and the land is level; you need to be resolute, brother. Before you depart, eat cardamoms and sandal as your feed. It is you to whom my words are addressed, do not tell them to anyone else. Cry out as you go, and make my rivals envious.

5 Full moon, you rise after decorating yourself in a thousand ways. But although you may employ a thousand contrivances, you can never equal the beloved. He surpasses your lifetime of beauty in an instant.

Many suns may rise, eighty-four moons may rise. I swear by God that without the beloved everything seems to be darkness. 6

Oh moon, how can I liken your beauty to the beloved? You shine white at night; the beloved is always bright. 7

Oh moon, I will tell you the truth, if you will not take it amiss. Sometimes you come up thin, sometimes you rise full. A fire blazes in your face, but it is not the equal of the beloved's forehead. 8

When he raised his eyes drunkenly and cast his graceful looks, the rays of the sun were lessened and the moon was dimmed. The stars of the Pleiades were humbled when they saw the beloved. Before the beloved's beauty, jewels lost their luster. 9

Oh bright morning star, you rise like him, and your brilliance at dawn matches the beloved's brightness. 10

Oh star, I often gaze at you, because you rise from the place where my beloved resides. 11

My beloved dwells in a distant place beneath that star. My beloved is as sweet as honey, he never turns bitter. 12

13 There are freckles, moles, and beauty spots on my beloved's face. Accursed are the nights I endure after he has gone.

14 Oh moon, as you rise, cast your first glance toward the beloved. In the name of God, tell of this wretch's state, of how my eyes every day watch the road in the hope of your coming.

15 Good moon, deliver my messages to my beloved. Rise over his courtyard. Speak softly, humbly touching his feet.

16 Rise, oh moon, and gaze on my beloved. He is near you but far from me. He lies sleeping in the cool night with his hair perfumed. I cannot get there on foot, and my father will not give me a camel to mount early in the morning and ride toward my beloved.

17 Lord, when in this life will you bring us together? Lovers' minds are where love's torment plays. My beloved is abroad; to whom shall I tell my secret?

18 My heart is thinking of my beloved; where will he be now? Darling, you do not come and step on to my bed. Now is the time for intimate talk, but to whom can I tell my secret?

I have no camel or horse to take me to my beloved by night, and I cannot get there on foot. I am helpless and sit shedding tears. 19

Camel, stop being lazy and step out. I need to get to where my beloved lives. I will feed you sandal, while the rest of the herd eats the *lāṇī*[1] bush. Move, camel, so that I may be with him tonight. 20

Young camel, stop being lazy and step out. The road to my beloved is straight, don't think it is crooked. Stop being so lazy, look sharp, and let us meet there tonight. 21

I took my camel and tied it to the tree so that it might feed on the buds. The perverse camel secretly ate the *lāṇī* bush. Mother, the way it behaves has driven me to distraction. 22

Today, oh camel, listen to my plea. Don't get anxious as you cross the land and water. Take me to the company of my beloved and let me be with him. 23

I decorate your neck with rubies and put pearl necklaces on it. Now I will place a silken saddlecloth over you and feed you lots of sandal if you get me there tonight. 24

25 Oh camel, I will put a leading rein of gold on you. I will feed you buds of sandal and bended branches of henna, if you deliver me to my beloved tonight.

26 My camel does not go with the herd to graze. It has been struck by the arrow of love, which has utterly destroyed it. It has given up all concern for its life and creeps along the path to the beloved.

27 It moves in the midst of the herd and grazes on sandalwood. Mother, I cannot see the footprints of my camel clearly. It seems to be at one with the world, but at heart it grazes over there.

28 Today the camel is behaving differently from yesterday. When it comes into the courtyard, it does not long for its nosebag. Perhaps it has grazed with the herd on some poisonous creeper.

29 The camel greedily thrust its mouth into the creepers. The owners of the field became aware of this, and the watchmen threatened it. The camel lost its courage, and not a sound emerged from its mouth. The wretched camel forgot its high spirits.

30 Twist strong ropes to tie up your camel. Sweet-smelling creepers are spread across the plain. Once the camel has got a taste for them, it will no longer stay put without a hobble rope.

To keep my camel still I put many hobbles on it. It dragged its ropes with it in order to graze on the *lāṇī*. Lord, set straight my camel's mind. In your mercy, make him right, says Latif. 31

I am tired of telling my camel not to go near the *ak*[2] plant. But it has become addicted to the creeper that has robbed many of their reason. Plenty of sandal trees grow all around. But this perverse beast has made me weep tears of blood. 32

Get up and and tie it tight; if it gets loose it will run free. If I feed it, it becomes refractory, so put a saddle on it. Hobble it so that it may graze and cry out. 33

It has hobbles on both forefeet and on both rear legs and chains of steel around its chest. Mother, my camel is in the habit of eating fresh flowers. Who can put a spell on it? It hardly stays with me. 34

Who has put a spell on you and led you astray, oh camel? You have blinkers on your eyes, and your feet are chafed by the oil press.[3] Have you forgotten your herd that was bound and used to turn the press? 35

It does not eat the white flowers of the *khaṭaṇahāru*[4] plant, and it spits out sandal juice. It does not go 36 near fragrant plants and takes no notice of the *sirkhanḍu*.[5] The taste of the *lāṇī* has driven the camel crazy.

37 Camel, you do not feed on sandal or drink fresh water. You do not go near fragrant plants and spit on fine food. Why do you delight in the *lāṇī* more than anything else in the world?

38 Two branches cost millions, and leaves cost half a million a quarter. That is what my camel eats every day.

39 Give millions to drive my precious camel. Put plenty of cardamoms in its feed. It will not argue at all when saddled, but will take me to my love.

40V Oh God, although you chase me away, I will not leave your door.
For me it is as good as seeing you, even if you do not show me your face.
I have seen many other doors, but you are the only one for me.

5 *Sirirag*

So that the beloved may think of you, do not remove the thought of him from your mind. Accept all his commands, so that you do not deprive yourself of his favor. 1

So that the beloved may think of you, keep thoughts of him in your mind. Wash and clean your sail and make it white with soap. Sailor, remain aware, so that you may get across. 2

So that the beloved may think of you, do not remove the idea of him from your mind. Destroy and get rid of false thinking from your heart. In this way you will be relieved of the terror of the other side. 3

So that the beloved may think of you, keep your mind fixed on him. In this way you will see the wealth of those lands in your telescope. Always keep your boat clean, sailor, and stay close to the pilot. 4

I dealt in glass, I did not deal in pearls. I did business in lead, says Shah. Such is my state; I rely upon your grace. 5

I traded in worthless glass and broke my contract with God. I filled my frame to the brim with sins. Fool, do you have any awareness of this? 6

7 You traded in worthless glass; arise and communicate with God. Remove deceit from your heart; truth is what pleases the lord. Oh jewel, light the fire of love in your mind. Arise and approach in such a way that your trade may be successful.

8 Turbid water, waves, white water, floods—there is no end to the water. God, do not let the boat collide with a sandbank. May no danger befall the boat, and may no damage affect its timber. May this poor craft not suffer any blow.

9 Their sails are straight, their rigging is new, and their sailors are skilled. The companions set out on their voyage over the ocean with a favorable wind. As they return with longing, may their boats be protected by your mercy.

10 Drops of water leaked through the planks. I saw the tears of those whose goods were ruined.

11 All that is in the world is dependent on your grace. There is no shortfall in your grace, says Latif. I cannot be saved by justice, so let your favor operate.

12 The ashes of those who spend the whole night awake in remembrance of God find honor, says Abdul Latif. Thousands come before them and offer their respects.

Offer your devotions to the sea, where so much water 13
flows. Hundreds of jewels, pearls, and rubies
lie within its depths. If you obtain the slightest
amount of that treasure, oh worshiper, you will
become rich.

The worshipers who offered their devotions to the 14
sea became rich. They brought bunches of gems
from the deep. In the waves, says Latif, they found
rubies beyond price, so precious is their value.

The ocean did not fight with those who were devoted 15
to God. Their repentance got them through the
storm. Holding to their trust in God, they easily
traversed the swift current. They had a perfect
pilot as their helper mid-ocean.

Those who are truly aware trade with the lord all night 16
long. With slavelike devotion those brave heroes
fill their boats. The champions cross the sea in an
instant.

Divers know the way to explore the ocean. They have 17
entered the depths and gathered gems. They have
brought up handfuls of diamonds and rubies and
given them away.

The divers have entered the white waves of the deep 18
sea. They have crossed the waters and entered the

pitch-dark whirlpools. Those who know the sea bring forth priceless gems.

19 Those who went into the sea with protective glass over their faces[1] entered the depths and sought out shells. They are the ones whose eyes will see priceless gems.

20 Muddy swamps and surging waters lie ahead; my boat cannot withstand the waves. It is loaded with the countless sins I have accumulated. They cannot be described; my sins are innumerable. Be merciful and get me across the dark shoals.

21 Be mindful of this deep water's current. Look at your neighbors and become concerned. Do you not see the world going toward the harbor on the far shore?

22 There is one thing in the mind of man; God does something else. It is the miracle of the lord that he rescues people from the deep whirlpool. It is the power of the lord that he takes the drowning out of the deep water.

23 There is one thing in the mind of man; God does something else. It is he who casts people into the whirlpool, and it is he who rescues you from the abyss. It is the power of the one God that he delivers everyone to a safe destination.

Trusting in the north wind, yesterday they unfurled 24
their sails from the mast. Oh God, may the blade
of their rudder not suffer any damage. The traders
have loaded their craft with merchandise.

Trade in the merchandise that does not become old by 25
being stored, and that does not incur the slightest
loss when sold abroad. Use your wealth to do
business that will bring you salvation.

Pilots gather and bring reports on waters close to 26
shore. But they provide no information on places
where the current rages.

Your boat is old, do not load it with too much 27
merchandise. There are holes in its bottom, and
water leaks through its sides. This time is gone;
think about the day that is to come.

There are holes in its bottom, water flows in through 28
its sides. Its mast is now old, and its rigging is all
loose. So long as the steersman is strong, it keeps
going against the current.

They stop its holes and oil its timbers every day. After 29
these preparations, says Shah, they launch it into
the sea. They twist strong ropes for the boat.
When they finally set sail, no danger befalls it.

30 Now you have come and seen the shore that you had only heard about. Asleep in the world, says Latif, you did not remember God at all. Heedlessly you have brought your boat into the whirlpool. Oh God, preserve this old craft that has been worn out by the swift current. We are weak, and our ship sails under your protection. Lord, deliver your company to Porbandar.[2]

31 Oh boat, go with the larger vessels. As you sail across to the other side, take strong equipment with you. The mighty sounds come from the ocean.

32 The boat is in the middle of the sea; will it drown or will it emerge safely? The pegs the carpenter fixed have all rotted. The pilots are not in their former place; Frankish pirates[3] have taken over. Sailor, robbers have come onto your boat. Where big boats have sunk, we trust in you to save us.

33 Boatman, you cannot manage to do both things. You sleep all night but have the rudder beside you. In the morning you will be asked to account for everything on the other side.

34 The currents are swift, and the boats cannot stay at anchor. Only with great difficulty can large craft progress against the current. The traders cast anchor weights into the waters. I have heard fearful reports from the pilots.

Trader, you will not be able to manage without the 35
lord of the sea. Oil the timbers of your boat and make it sound. The sea strikes the sides of the boats. The tide will attack those whose accounts fall short.

The sailor who keeps watch delivers reports to the 36
captain. By God's grace those who are carefully equipped for the voyage pass through the storm, says Latif. Remembering God, they have got back from Aden.[4]

Oh helmsman, do not sleep when there is danger in 37
the harbor. The whirlpools near the shore are churning like curds in a pot. Do not sleep and put yourself through such suffering.

All lie asleep, trusting in the captain. You too can 38
sleep, oh watchman, for there is no danger in the harbor. Those whom the lord protects will pass safely through all difficulties.

Entrust all that you do to God. Turn your will 39
completely over to him and let go of your sorrows and cares. In his mercy, the almighty will help you succeed.

The good perform good deeds, the evil commit 40
evil. They each behave in accordance with their natures.

41 He loads the baggage onto the camels and calls to those who are exhausted. It is the way of the beloved to make sure that the caravan reaches its destination.

42 If you recognize the value of doing business, you will do nothing else. Learn about this from the traders, from whose hands you may most humbly gain pearls.

43 Do not offer priceless gems to those who do not understand the business. Deal in gems only where you find a proper jeweler. Those whose business is with gold reject worthless glass.

44 Oh gold, go to a proper dealer and do not do anything else. Abandon the trade in which there are no jewels.

45 Oh gold, if the dealers move on, you should move on too. Nobody else will value you properly; they will take you and put you next to a brass pot.

46 Glass is bought and jewels are rejected. I hold truth wrapped in my hem, but I am utterly ashamed to offer it.

47 Those jewelers are gone who used to pierce diamonds and rubies. Those who have come after them do not even know the value of lead. In the places

where they used to be, blacksmiths now hammer base metals.

May those jewelers who assess precious gems not depart! They put a loupe in their eye and assess all of them. They determine the value of a pearl's quality from its circumference. Without the expert eye of the dealer, the value of the gem is at risk. 48

Touched by a woman, the jewel was broken in its box. When perfect, says Shah, it was worth thousands. Later, when broken, its value was more than a billion.[5] 49

The place where there are jewels is where thieves gather. Those who keep their precious treasure safe are extremely fortunate. 50

The thief[6] keeps saying: "I am the one whom eighty eyes cannot find when I am hidden." 51

There are waves without number, dangerous shores, and dark whirlpools, white breakers on the deep sea, and a powerful swell is running. Get up, oh heedless one, or the water will overwhelm you. 52

Yesterday large and powerful ships were cast into the whirlpool. Today it is your vessel on which the waters have set their sights. 53

54 Never let your mind be unaware of the dangers of the sea. Sailor, be alert, although you delight in sleeping. Stay awake and sail your vessel over the water to the other side.

55 Boatman, sail your vessel across the waves. Those who know about the deep lament the dangers of the sea. Take the advice of the experts so that you may cross the ocean.

56 Experts deliver reports of the turbulent ocean. They do not go near falsehood but only deal in truth. Their business is with the helplessness that comes in the middle of the night. They bring the whole company safely across the sea.

57 They put cloves, cardamoms, fine clothes, and lustrous pearls aboard. They placed valuable stores in its bottom. In its rigging, says Latif, they tied floral decorations. As they went aboard, they made offerings to the holy Prophet, that he might in his mercy preserve the boats that they sailed on the swift current.

58 In the evening I sit and pray to the ocean, saying: "May the boat reach harbor and may my beloved come home!" This is my concern. May they all be happy, like the trader with his merchandise. By the grace of the Prophet, they were not stopped

by the customs officers. The sailors who voyaged afar have entered their own country.

Pull your raft into shallow water and tie it up there. No 59
one else will bring it to you in the deep ocean.

Seek out the generous lord and do not sit there 60
carelessly. Be alert all the time—lightning strikes suddenly.

The lightning strikes, but unluckily you have been 61
overcome by sleep. Those who are not fearful for themselves are lost.

Sailor, be alert and keep a tight hold on the rudder. 62
A mighty wind blows and the Indus is turbulent. Those who are filled with thoughts of self are lost.

The stars have no rest, the rivers have no peace. You 63
are content with what you get. What can you know of true wealth, when you sleep through every night?

The ways to God are difficult and hard to travel. Even 64
those who belong to that country get confused. Enter the white breakers that confront you with profound love.

In your body, search hard for the vessel of his mercy. 65
Fasten tight the sails of devotion and sincerity.

Weigh the merchandise of prayers and put it
aboard. Then your boat will not be lost before it
gets to Aden.

66 Those who offer their devotions to the sea gather
jewels. Those who search the shallows only find
conches and shells.

67V Your companions have loaded up, oh. Your eyes are
full of sleepiness.
Your neighbors have cast off their anchors in the
middle of the ocean.
The ferry is full, your turn has come.
You eat your fill, then you sleep all night
unconsciously.
Have your ears not heard the announcement of
departure?
It is the time for speedy repentance; this is true
awareness.
Listen, dear brother, do not sleep so much.
The lord sent you for the truth; you are false as you
stand in line.
Have your ears not heard the roar of the whirlpool?
I enter the water without a pot,[7] putting my trust in
God.
Keep me safe, merciful God, from the doubts of those
who do not believe.
Every soul shall have a taste of death:[8] recite this advice.
You are the prey the falcon hunts, yet think yourself a
hunter.

On that day brother will flee from brother[9] is what it
says in scripture.
My boat is in deep water; come to me, oh my refuge.
So many moments were lost, so many thousands of
opportunities were wasted.
If you had given them to God, perhaps you would have
crossed safely.
In your house you gathered riches, which came up to
your knees.
It is called carrion[10] in the Traditions; this is the
likeness for the dark world.
You did not share it with the poor or fear the wrath of
God.
She runs from her husband, so how can she go with
you?
Life does not last forever; listen to this carefully.
Oh forgetful one, do not forget the terror of the
grave's walls.

6 *Samundi*

1 Stay beside the sailors' anchor cable, woman, in case they raise anchor and leave you, casting your heart into distress.

2 Languish beside their anchor cable, mother, in case the sailors raise anchor and leave you, setting your heart on fire.

3 Sit beside their anchor cable, mother. The sailors will travel abroad, while you walk about unawares. Why do you not go with those whose homeland is the ocean?

4 The oar cannot push my heart away from the anchor. My merciful beloved has captured my heart with his fine qualities.

5 Those were the days of my youth, when my beloved departed on his travels. Though I weep, my beloved does not stay. Mother, what can I do? The trader has put me on a pyre and set sail.

6 There are no boats at the landing place, nor traders in conversation. Today, my friends, I am suffering from the wounds inflicted by the sailors. Separation from my beloved, oh my neighbors, is killing me.

7 He has sailed away and left me completely abandoned. Ages have passed, but no one has returned. Oh

wretched girl, the pain caused by the one who has
departed will kill you.

Mother, the sailors who sailed away to the deep ocean 8
never came back. Perhaps the swift current of the
sea flowed over them.

May they arrive back at the harbors from which they 9
sailed. Oh lord, may a favorable wind bring those
sailors home.

Love for a sailor is mingled with grief. The trader 10
sailed away, leaving my body on the gallows.

"May you forget the trade that you have learned. You 11
only arrived yesterday, but you are already getting
ready to travel."[1]

Holding on to the oar post, she weeps, with her hands 12
on the prow and saying: "Accursed be the trade,
beloved, that you have learned."

She does not let him row away but holds fast to the 13
oar. "Stay for me tonight, my dear. Oh beloved, do
not forsake me and go on such a long voyage."

"Perhaps my love was weak, for him to embark and 14
leave me standing there. I made no advance plan
to go with the sailors. Otherwise I would have put
myself in the boat and coiled the rope around me."

15 Do not fall in love with those who wander in boats. When they sail out to sea, the women standing on the shore suffer pain.

16 “Like a boat in a bad harbor, my heart has been in a bad way for days. My beloved has never bothered to ask after me.”

17 “The ends of the grasses are full blown, and the north wind blows. Come to me, beloved. I have made thousands of vows for your return, my husband.”

18 “If he comes now, I will enjoy myself in conversation with him. Mother, may I embrace my beloved and talk with him.”

19 “Mother, if my beloved comes, I will quarrel with him, saying: ‘You took many days to come, but you told me that they would be few.’”

20 As soon as he gets off the boat he talks about leaving, giving me over to grief and casting my heart into the current.

21 “Restore me to life by talking about my beloved. Today rebuild my heart, which has fallen apart like the collapsed tower of a fort.”

22 The flags of the rich merchants look dazzling in every direction. Mother, the sailors have returned,

making a fine display. The crow[2] has been talking about them since yesterday.

Today the traders talk about going. My beloved is going to leave, and will not stay even if I weep. How can I stop the sailors, mother? They have raised their anchors and sailed their boats out into deep water. 23

I cannot get him out of my mind; oh God, may he not forget me. My deepest being is intertwined with him. 24

There is sweet talk at the landing place, mother; the sailors have arrived. The traders' words give me new life. 25

They left when the north wind was blowing, and they return on the spring breeze. I want nothing to do with the sailors' trade. For those whose courtyards they enter, today is a happy Eid. 26

If he enters my courtyard, friends, I am filled with joy. I give to others the precious gems that I vowed to my beloved. 27

They mended their sails on the harbor quays. When these were patched and fixed, they erected the masts. At sea they flew their flags. They passed over the waves by God's grace, says Latif. 28

29 They mended their sails on the harbor quays. They sought news from the master mariners and sailed away. They sought safe harbor, and did not wander off course to an unsafe place.

30 There are harbors in every land, but precious gems are not found on sandy shores. Priceless jewels are given by those who are dressed like fakirs.

31 The traders' wives stand at the landing place and make offerings. They bring musk and offer it to the ocean.[3]

32 She lights lamps on water and dry land, she ties flags on trees and plants,[4] saying: "Oh God, my hope is that my husband may come."

33 She who performs pilgrimage to the water and does not offer lamps should not desire her husband's return.

34 "If I go I may get there, but the harbor is far away. I have no money on me to pay for my passage. Boatman, tell me how I can get to my beloved. I call out standing at your door, sailor."

35 The travelers had nothing on them, nor did the boatmen take them on board for nothing. They remained on the shore all day long until the sun set. When the lord helped them, they reached safe harbor, says Shah.

"I have borrowed utensils and put them on to cook. The cold winds of winter have begun. Sighs arise within me as I look at the other women's husbands."[5] 36

I stood at the landing place, and my beloved sailed away. There must be some serious fault in me, for otherwise he is very kind. 37

I stand at the landing place, and my beloved has set sail. He has gone, placing his trust in God, and I will keep praying for him all the time. I will not lose the hope that he will come back to me. 38

After crossing the salty sea, they returned on the sweet waters of the river. Major traders do not deal in gold. What they desire are the pearls of the Indus. Wealthy sailors have returned from ransacking Lanka.[6] 39

"Lanka, Lanka" is all that those who have set out for Lanka can think of. When they hear of Lanka's gold, the sailors have no peace. At dawn they unfurl their sails and cross the salty sea. Those who went away for business return richly rewarded. 40

The traders have again unfurled their sails at dawn. When I see their oars, my heart is upset. I will die, mother, when I think of the sailors. 41

42 Oh mother of your sailor son, you do not stop him going. He has returned in the twelfth month since he started and again he thinks of traveling.

43 It would have been better for me not to have married a sailor. As soon as the north wind blows, my beloved talks about going.

44 If you, my husband, were a trader, I should never have got married to you. You are planning to travel abroad after spending only twenty-four hours with me.

45 Seeing that it is Diwali,[7] the sailors prepare their sails. The trader's wife embraces her husband and weeps. Wretched woman, the pangs caused by your husband will attack you at dawn.

46V Mother, what can I do? My love cannot remain unchecked.
My trader has set off, placing me on a pyre.
My marriage to a sailor makes me weep day and night.
Like termites, my sorrows have consumed me right up to my topknot.
Sorrows have wrapped themselves around my heart like creepers.
Mother, with humbly folded hands I will go to my guide.

7 *Suhini*

The current is strong, the canals flow strongly, but the flow of love is extraordinarily strong. Those whose love is for God the Profound are absorbed in thoughts of closeness. Lord, bring back the one who has captured my heart. 1

Fresh streams flow before me here; ahead of me the mighty river flows. You sit at home in comfort, friends, safe in your husbands' care. But if you once caught sight of Sahar's lovely face, then perhaps you would not try to hold me back, but would all plunge in with your pots. 2

Many women stand on the bank and proclaim their love with cries of "Sahar, Sahar!" Some care about their lives, some say they are sacrificed to him and plunge in. Sahar belongs to those who happily plunge in. 3

Crows sit crouched in the trees as the day draws to its close. When she hears the evening call to prayer, she goes to seek the spots where her dear Sahar dwells. 4

She grasps her pot and enters the river, looking long at its twists and turns. *How right it is to sacrifice one's head at the beloved's feet.*[1] This is the mystery of union. Lord, deliver safely across all those whose time of ecstasy is the night. 5

6 She grasps her pot and enters the river, looking long at its twists and turns. She has arrived at the place of *whoever fears the place of the lord*.[2] Shah says: No fearful place will stop lovers filled with longing. Lord, safely deliver across all those whose time of ecstasy is the night.

7 She grasps her pot and plunges in, putting her trust in God. The alligator grasps her leg, the cayman has her head. Her bracelets mingle with the mud, the current grabs her hair. Countless creatures cling closely to her, and river monsters maul her body. Whole schools of fish surround her, as Suhini is severed limb from limb.

8 It was good that the pot broke, and good that my bracelets snapped. *How heroic are those who seek the lord*,[3] the only raft for all who drown. My husband, Dam, is false and foul; in my heart I hold Mehar.

9 It was good that the pot broke; it was actually an obstacle. The instrument plays in my being, the rebab dwells in my spirit. Without Sahar, I would give up great virtue.

10 It was good that the pot broke, oh my heart, so swim for a while. I keep my eyes controlled every day. The chief of the herdsmen has shown me the straight path.

It was good that the pot broke; do not give up hope. 11
The raft of *Do not despair of God's mercy*[4] is the
one for you to swim with. Desire for the beloved
will let you behold Mehar's face.

Once her pot fell to pieces, her props were gone and 12
the woman died. But it was then that Suhini heard
the calls of her Mehar.

Do not take your self with you, forget your props. 13
Love will take you through the torrent and get
you safely across. Let yourself be supported by
longing, if you would reach the other side.

Set off without your self, and go without any aids. Use 14
steps of love to travel across the water, Suhini.
Take love's name and go to the side where the
beloved lives.

There is no greater support than love in the heart. 15
Insincere women stand on this bank and demand
a raft. For those who go without one, the river
turns into a mere stream. Actually, it is love that
gets lovers to their destination. Whirlpools do not
stop those who seek Mehar.

They seek so hard to find Mehar, but it is Mehar who 16
looks for them. For all who feel the force of love, a
raft is only a handicap.

17 Sahar is the same as Suhini, and it is Sahar who is the sea. This mystery is magical, this puzzle is profound.

18 There were many loudly roaring whirlpools and crocodiles in the waters where she hurled herself and was carried by the current. Through divine favor she crossed the waves, says Latif.

19 Fearful is the force of the river, where there are mighty monsters. There are countless crocodiles in the water, terrifying in their thousands. "I do not think I have any strength in my body apart from you," she cries. "Lord Sahar, who hides all faults, come quickly to me in the torrent."

20 Fearful is the force of the river, where the whirlpools roar. Suhini is among the wild river creatures, and the waves roll over her. "Come quickly and with kindness, oh Sahar my beloved," she cries. "Oh my guide, give me your hand, and rescue me from the deep."

21 Fearful is the force of the river, where the whirlpools roar. The terror of the far bank fills my heart. Love destroys the force of the current, says Shah. Oh lord, be kind to me, and in your mercy let me cross over.

Fearful is the force of the river, where many creatures dwell. Sailors cannot plumb the depths of the water. Wild beasts roam roaring in the river. In the deep water entire boats go under, and not a trace is found of their timbers. No one who enters those terrible whirlpools emerges from them. Oh Sahar, help those who cannot swim to get across. 22

There is tumult and uproar in the river, where the waves crash. Hundreds of people with floats are aghast when they enter the water. Those who truly can swim think it requires only a single leap to get across. 23

To enter the water quickly is the act of the determined. Ten times a day Dam taunts me. Reason, sense, and modesty are all three destroyed by love. 24

Without looking for a safe place, she finds nowhere to enter the river. Filled with desire for Sahar, she has one thought upon another. In the dark night and surrounded by whirlpools, she is distressed by fantastic thoughts. The pain caused by her beloved makes the river seem of no account to her. 25

She enters where she will; only insincere girls inspect the riverbank. Only in appearance is her body 26 with Dam; her heart is joined with Mehar. In her desire for Sahar she thinks the river is a ditch.

27 Her route lies in whichever direction the river flows; only insincere girls inspect the riverbank. Those who are filled with desire for Sahar do not ask about entry points or landing places. Those who thirst for love think the river is a mere step.

28 It does not matter where she enters from, difficult places become easy. Suhini crosses safely, unaffected by the whirlpools. Her eyes are filled with the brightness of her beloved. The true lord did right by her, because her search for him was true.

29 From the very first, Todi[5] was a seeker of the lord. She had no boat or boatman, nor had she tied herself a rope. The middle of the river seemed knee-deep to her.

30 From the beginning Todi was favored by love. Around her neck she wore her beloved's garland of honor. The landing place she found is the support of all the world.[6]

31 Abandon that love which makes you happy, Todi. Away from Sahar, insincere girls put on proud airs. Great is your error if you spend your days with Dam.

First learn the lesson of the Law, Suhini. The truth of 32
Reality far surpasses the Way. It is Gnosis[7] that is the real task of lovers.

Patience is found in the dwelling places of the 33
grateful. Those who have been joined with him in union do not disclose anything about it. Those whose hearts have been destroyed swim across without any help.

She enters the water while the rain falls on the 34
midwinter night. Let us go and ask Suhini what she knows of love. For twenty-four hours a day she bears only Mehar in her mind.

Everyone enters the water in Savan; she is happy in 35
winter. In the torrent of her love she hurls her body into the deep water. There is no justice in the river, which kills lovers.

Oh river, do not wear away these overhanging banks, 36
you too will be held to account. The days of Savan will not be here forever. By tomorrow your floods will subside.

The fires of my beloved Mehar burn in my heart. 37
The burning power of love casts those whom it consumes into the torrent. For those who know about Sahar the river is as smooth as the desert.

38 "Sisters, the bells stir my whole body. How can I disclose to all and sundry the love that their clappers have aroused? The beloved to whose branch I cling sends me his support."

39 Black are the eddies and black is the night, in which the black snakes hiss. Both banks of the wild Indus are threatening. The waves strike her as she goes across to Sahar. She is guided in midstream by the tinkling of the bells.

40 "Remembering my beloved is what keeps me alive. What will he do with me when I find him? My being overflows with thoughts of him. He cannot be separated from me, for he pervades my whole heart.

41 The sound of the bells in the river thickets arouses me. My dormant feelings for my beloved Mehar are stirred. I will collapse at his camp on the far bank.

42 I heard the sound of the bells on the far bank as I slept. They stirred my consciousness and filled me with the desire for his camp. I swear to God that the fragrance of my beloved Mehar has reached me. Let me go and see my dear one face to face.

43 Where is Mehar, and where are the bells tinkling? Where is my beloved's bonfire, and where is the far bank? I have spent my whole life thrashing through the water to reach it."

She drank a draught of love from Mehar.[8] The taste of that drink intoxicated her. She was struck by the arrow of love, which is sharper than steel, says Latif. 44

"May Mehar never die, and may his byre never be bare. May the hair of the heifers' herdsman never be twisted.[9] Sahar is my glory, though men taunt me because of him." 45

The herds grazed the pasture, then crossed the river and came to an island.[10] By God's grace, says Latif, they will pass over the flood. 46

The herds grazed the pasture and crossed the river, avoiding the whirlpools. Thousands will raise their heads in relief, as guaranteed by Sahar. Safe and happy, the buffaloes will get across. 47

There is nothing but the river as far as the eye can see; the other bank is far away. The crazy woman enters the waves, where there is danger to her life. When creatures overwhelmed by the torrent see their faults, they are overwhelmed. If you grant them your mercy, no one is in the power of the current. 48

It is easy for lovers, even if the river rages. In the end their hearts cannot rest without the torrent. Going toward Sahar, they will sacrifice their lives. Sahar is the helper of those who love him. 49

50 Realize that those who enter the water will get across. If you leap into the wild Indus, Mehar will be with you as your float.

51 Shah says: Those whose eyes are fixed on Mehar's face may plunge into the deep water without a float, and the river cannot drown them.

52 "The torrent rages where my heart's desire is strongest. There the swift current roars. Bring me to Mehar in the waves, says Latif.

53 My pure love cannot be checked, however much I try. Overcome by the surge of passion, I enter the water and sacrifice my life. To go there is a duty for those who have Mehar in their hearts."

54 She has absolutely no fear of Dam. She does not let the water wet her clothes. For the sake of Mehar the woman crosses the eddies in the dark night.

55 "Sisters, come to me when people lie in unbroken sleep, for I am troubled by thoughts of my beloved. If anyone speaks against me, I take their taunts as a compliment."

56 If Suhini had not entered the river, how would she ever have been heard of? She would not have spent much time in this life. It was the drink of milk he gave her that made her crazy.[11] Shah

says that it was love that killed her. She would have died anyway, but she was doubly rewarded through drowning.

The whirlpools whisper to one another at dawn, saying: "In the middle of the night her eyes long for the water. Although they are given draughts to drink, still their thirst is not quenched." 57

How can the fish that is always in the river stink? Its only worry is "Where can I drink water?" 58

All the waves are rubies, and the current smells sweeter than musk. Many scents of ambergris come to her from the water. Yesterday, longing for her beloved, Suhini plunged into the eddies. 59

"Tell on the riverbank what you saw in the deep. There is a great abundance of water; do not let your hem get wet. If you keep thinking of Sahar, you will get across safely. 60

Only Sahar can undo the knot he tied in my heart. Oh God who listens to all, let me be joined to Sahar, so that this knot may be undone." 61

Sahar's beauty preceded the writing of fate. There was no *Be and it was*,[12] nor any other idea. Suhini's song came before the angels were created. It was then that she fell in love with Mehar, says Latif. 62

63 Suhini found her entry point and crossed over the river to Mehar before the time of the covenant. She was true to the mystery of *"Am I not your lord?" and they said,* "*Yes.*"[13] She saw the path of the beloved's love and she showed it to others.

64 I have been married to Mehar from the time of the covenant, when God said, *"Am I not?"* to the souls. How can anyone turn back what has been ordained in the book of fate?

65 From the time when God the One declared, *"Am I not?"* to the souls, her heart was drawn to Mehar and she desired to love him. Fate broke her pot in half in the current of the river. In its depths, the woman fulfilled what had been decreed for her by destiny.

66 From the time when almighty God aroused the souls with *"Am I not?"* she has been in search of the straight path, says Shah. Only a few among millions experience the valley of oneness. Many are swept away by the delusion of the river.

67 "I burn, I am grilled, I am roasted, I writhe, I yearn. My body's thirst for my beloved is not sated by drinking. If I were to swallow a whole ocean, it would not make a single mouthful."

68 The night is dark, her pot is unbaked, it is the twenty-ninth night of the lunar cycle. There is no trace of

the moon, the river is in spate. Suhini has come for Sahar at midnight. This is divinely ordained; why else would anyone enter the whirlpools?

The night is dark, her pot is unfired, she has no float 69
with her. For the sake of her beloved she dives in without delay. Love makes the Indus seem like a bare plain.

It was not on this bank or on that one, but in the 70
middle of the river that the poor girl swam. Her beloved is on dry land by the river's edge, all the rest is deep water. Plunge in, do not look around you; he shows his mercies to those who drown.

It was not on this bank or on that one, but in the 71
middle of the river that the poor girl swam. She plunges in without looking at the pot, which got a hole in it. Oh God, bring her to safety from the raging river.

Thousands of oceans roar, but still Suhini's constancy 72
is unshaken. Is that how true love is broken?

Do not set your hand on the beloved's raft as you 73
drown. In the morning he will say to you: "We delivered you across."

Even if you are drowning, do not touch the beloved's 74
raft. If you think you will reach the beloved,

then go with the current against you. Step in the direction where there is no safety hut.

75 Sahar is the savior of those who drown on dry land. He puts them on his shoulders, says Latif, and takes them through the waves. He delivers those who embark on lengthy quests as if the beloved were near.

76 If you drown in preparation for dry land, then go ahead and drown. Do not gather straw and thorn and sticks to make a raft. Otherwise there will be no call from Sahar, nor will Suhini be heard.

77 What you consider to be poems are divine verses.[14] They direct the mind toward the beloved.

78 Lord, it is you who drowns and you who saves, no one else has any power or claim. My condition is known to Mehar. Save the honor of this pot that is entering the whirlpool.

79 The herons are her pallbearers and the current is her bier. The cranes that live on the eyots offer their shoulders to carry her. When the recording angels[15] looked at her, her desire was fixed on Mehar.

80 Standing at the landing place, Mehar calls out to the boatmen: "I will lend a hand, if you will cast

your nets. If we trawl the depths, we may find my beloved."

Seizing the reeds on the riverbank, the lover stands and sighs: "My friend, why did you drown my beloved Suhini? Oh river, I shall complain against you on the day of resurrection." 81

Where the eddies whirl, where the whirlpools churn, swimmers did not find their rope, sailors did not plumb the depth. Many who do have floats stand trembling on the bank. How did you come to the place to plunge in from, you foolish girl? 82

Standing on the far bank, he calls to me, saying: "Come!" Not only is the deep water flowing fast, but also the waves are turbulent and the wind is blowing. I realize that those who have God as their helper will not drown. 83

Foolish girl, recognize Sahar on the far bank. Get rid of fantasy, fancy, and fear. Make your heart a mirror, and behold him in your heart. Proceed along this path, to enjoy the experience of seeing him. 84

The one for whom I search stands on the far bank. My beloved has taken my heart, roping it to himself. 85

86 Those who are drowning cleverly grasp the bushes. See how well the reeds behave, says Latif. Either they take those who grasp them to the bank or they go with them in the current.

87 The tender blades of the reed take those who are drowning out of the deep water. Either they take them across, says Latif, or they lament them from the start. Reeds are deservedly well known for saving people. Either they give support to those who are drowning or they go with them in the current.

88 You must depart to the other side; construct your raft for the deep water. These turbulent waves have held back the bravest of heroes, says Latif. They have been stopped in the middle of the river. But those who have experienced the Indus refuse to rest on its islands.

89 She goes with an unbaked pot and she does not ask for one that has been fired. She crosses the turbulent water, says Latif, and goes to her herdsman. How can she overcome the love by which she is herself overcome?

90 Suhini was happy when she saw the designs drawn by the potter. The water washed away the pattern and the glaze could not withstand the impact. In

her thoughtless youthful pride, Suhini thought it
was fully fired. In the Indus she came to know that
it was unbaked.

"So what if it is unfired? The favor of my beloved is 91
firm. Sahar is my beloved, it is wrong for me to
look at Dam. Whether squalls or strong winds
blow, I will go on to the far bank."

The unfired pot was quite unable to withstand 92
the river and it crumbled into pieces. She lost
her strength in the stream, her arms became
exhausted. Pouring in from all sides, the waves
buried her. Her heart was filled with the reality
of the angel of death.

The pot deceived her, its designs drove her mad. 93
"Alas, alas, Suhini is drowning," the waves
lamented. The unfired pot killed the lovely girl
in the waves.

Take with you a fired pot with fine designs. Return the 94
unfired pot straight to the potter. Suhini, hear in
your heart what the lord commands. Or else the
waves of the Indus will deceive and destroy you.

"I am lost, my kind beloved, come back to me. Except 95
for you, lord, I have no aid or support. It is up to
Sahar if he gets people out of the deep river."

96 It is Sahar's favor that will get them out of the deep river. We will find support from no one else there. Mehar, grant me an escape from the torrent.

97 A single loud cry[16] is heard in the water and on dry land, and in the forests and plains. All things deserve the gallows. They all make thousands of Mansurs; which ones will you hang?

98 Thoughts of the beloved are everywhere, and Punhun is present everywhere. The whole land is Mansur; how many of him will you slaughter?

99 The waves have thousands of forms, although water is the same to look at. Abandon the idea of fathoming the deep. Where love has no limit, destroy your desire. If you stop searching for landing places, you will get near to the beloved.

100 If I do not return home and perhaps spend time with him without him telling me to, I shall surely die beside my beloved's bonfire. It is not his form or his beauty that has driven me crazy. It is said that separation outweighs being together. That is why I turn around and swim back.

101 If my beloved comes to me on the day of resurrection, that is quite near. The glad news of being together sounds more distant than that.

How could I have known the danger of plunging into the water? How can anyone avoid the destiny decreed by God? Fate and love combined to thrust me into the waves. 102

It is not the reed or the pen that is to blame. Fate was written where no arm can reach. To whom should I complain when destiny moved the pen? 103

There is no limit to suffering, there is no limit to love. Love cannot be calculated, it knows its own limit. 104

The love I bear for you within me, my darling, cannot be grasped. My skin is burned in the oven of love and is set on fire. My beloved has pierced a hole in my heart without an awl. 105

Either let me swim myself or deliver me across. Either let me try myself or make an effort for me. Do not place a barrier in my way, oh my husband, for I am alone. 106

Many days have passed since I saw him; how can I know who he is? Many suns have set while I longed for him. Years have passed without him, away from whom I cannot stand a single moment. 107

Away from Sahar, Suhini is utterly impure. In the place where he lives, her impurity is destroyed. She becomes pure when she is beside the milk drinker.[17] 108

109 Away from Sahar, Suhini is unclean. She never washes her face with this water. If she was with her beloved, Suhini would bathe herself.

110 Away from Sahar, Suhini is feeble. She has developed a fever; alas for the wretched woman's state. Weak and without beauty, she is sick and heaves bitter sighs.

111 Away from Sahar, Suhini is in pain. She is sick when with Dam, but healthy with the herdsman. The medicine for Suhini's body is to see him. If she sees Mehar's face, she immediately becomes well.

112 Love rages at me every day. Beloved, why do you not come and restrain it?

113 So long as she was alive, she was ill and never rested for a moment. She entered the earth, yearning for her beloved.

114 So long as she was alive, she never sat at ease. After she was dead, she was enfolded by the waves and taken to Mehar.

115 Blessed is the dark night, accursed is the moonlight. May I not see anyone else between me and Mehar.

116 It was not the river, or a pond, or a lake, that drowned Suhini. Even after death, she went to Mehar with longing in her eyes.

Far more abundant than the rains of Savan or the grains of sand in the desert are the countless favors he has shown me. 117

Without my beloved, of what account am I?[18] 118V
Oh slave, flee from sin, not that there is profit in virtue.
There is nothing in piety, nothing in the rebab.[19]
You will become good in yourself, if you get rid of impurity.
Even the impure become pure, if they are attached to the divine court.
What the dust contains you will not find in anything else.[20]
The sparkles on the water are all only bubbles.
On your way toward the other side, humbly cling to the guide's stirrup.
Swift eagle, use your talons to catch the thief.[21]
By going along in a veil, do not lose sight of the beloved.
The self is subdued in union, like the inflectional vowels in assimilation.[22]
For the beloved's sake let yourself be roasted, swallowing annihilation.
Give the nectar of paradise to those who yearn for wine.
These are all the responses of one who is destroyed by love.

8 *Sasui Abiri*

1 Though love has consumed her, Sasui is still filled with love. The love she drank with Punhun is quite unbroken. Drinking from this spring itself increases her thirst.

2 Those who have drunk a drop from the ocean of his beauty are filled with boundless and unfathomed longing. Their desire is quite unaffected, although they are always in the deep water.

3 Those who bear love in their hearts are filled with profound thirst. Drink the cup of love, and arouse a greater thirst. Punhun, give me a drink, and quench my thirst with yet more thirst.

4 Those whose hearts are filled with love burn with a strange fire that brings them no joy. They wander in the wilderness, but their journey has no end. They die of thirst, though they are always in the deep water.

5 They are always in the deep water, but their inner thirst is not relieved. The sight of the beloved entails journeying through the wilderness. They die of thirst, though they are always in the deep water.

It is good that Sasui has accepted the wilderness for the sake of her beloved. Water itself is thirsty for those who thirst within.[1] 6

Their huts are beside the water, but the fools die of thirst. The beloved is closer than their breath, but they do not find the one they desire. They do not recognize their breath, but utter sad cries like travelers who are lost. 7

When she was near Punhun, Sasui did not understand. When she was close to Punhun, her true identity was revealed. The Brahman girl[2] lost her false sense of self among the Baloch.[3] 8

A hot wind blew and everyone was scorched. From the skies came the sweet scent of "Ah, ah!" The birds cried after the departure of Punhun. The pain reached the shepherd when he saw the state of the animals. In their great grief the beasts accepted death. The desert itself cried out in longing for Punhun. 9

Be led by helplessness, and follow in its footsteps. Friendless one, do not send reproaches to Kech. Put self aside, Sasui, and take love with you. Do not go near Azazil.[4] Take despair with you, then you may come near to hope. 10

11 Do not sit in Bhambhor, oh girl, but do not go to the Harho.[5] Never tell a lie, but do not reveal the truth. Do not suffer for the beloved, but do not forget the pain, Sasui.

12 Do not be glad in happiness, or fear when you see sorrow. Do not destroy your house, oh girl, or have it fixed. You are destroyed, but do not die in case you bring yourself to life.

13 Oh slave girl, do not slow down when you see the rocks. Gird your loins, says Latif, and hurry after the Kechis.[6] Go forward, Sasui, in awareness of the love inspired by the Baloch. Never abandon your hopes of that gracious lord. The beloved is nearer to you than your eyes; do not call him distant.

14 Those who turned their attention from this world to the next reached their goal. The beloved who possesses perfect beauty and understanding is less than a step away.

15 As my beloved went, perhaps he remembered me in the Vankar.[7] Sisters, today I have set out on my journey quickly and alone, so as to reach Kech by the favor of the Baloch.

16 I did not know the Vankar and did not bring any water with me. The mountain is cruel and very hot. The

hot wind blows on the helpless ones, says Latif. I am alone, my beloved, draw near to me.

The trees of the Vankar are tall, where dark blue snakes can be seen. There, says Abdul Latif, those who are left on their own must make great efforts. Oh guide, come to the path of those who have no family or tribe. 17

The poor girl had never seen the Vankar before. The people there had no kindness; all was darkness. Oh my girlfriends, she fell in love with the camel man for the sake of suffering. 18

You have left Punhun behind, but you search for your beloved in the mountains. You suffer hardships now that you are his wife. You have done wrong, poor woman, in looking for him in the wilderness. Your Hôt is not in the Harho; go back and ask those who sit there. Go back and ask them where Punhun is. Spend your whole life, poor woman, searching for him within yourself. 19

The man of the hills[8] is not where you thought, you foolish girl. Do not travel to the hills, the Vankar is inside you. Have nothing to do with strangers, but ask yourself where the beloved is. 20

Sasui, search all the corners of your house. Do not go far to look, the beloved is inside. 21

22 He is the one you have taken with you, Sasui, and he is the one whom you seek. Roaming about is not the way to gain awareness of him. Ask yourself about the beloved, so that you may find him there.

23 The one you seek far away is always with you. Oh helpless girl, says Latif, look for the beloved within yourself. Search within for a sign of him, for his resting place is inside you.

24 Why go to the Vankar, why not search for him here? The Baloch is not to be found anywhere else, says Latif. Be strong, gird your loins, and keep faith with Punhun. Look deep within yourself, the beloved's abode is inside you.

25 Go to your Hôt with your heart, do not travel on foot. Do not look for his tracks in the sand of the hills, Sasui, but proceed spiritually.

26 I ask you: "How should I travel to find the Kechis?" "Forget yourself and go into the desert," I say. "You wretched girl, do not stop longing for your beloved."

27 Do not let yourself forget your love, you wretched girl. Be as close as twins when they are born.

28 Do not let yourself forget your love, you wretched girl. Rub it on your face like a piece of musk.

How will girls who lack true passion get to the 29
Vindar?[9] Those who have thousands of different
desires remain stuck halfway.

"Everyone is full of desires, no one puts up with 30
hunger. No ordinary person can move along this
path. Any woman who does not hold her life dear
can travel with me."

Turn back, you married women, I will not return 31
without my husband. I will explore every inch of
this mighty mountain. Nothing can separate me
from my love for the camel man.

Go back, all of you who have husbands. The tale of 32
parting and separation is said to be a grievous one.
It is those who have a fire burning within them
who will cross the mountain.

Today, mother, I will wash my clothes and color them 33
with ochre. I will become a yogi, mother, do not
try to stop me. For the sake of my Hôt Baloch, I
will wear large rings in my ears.[10]

Did my brothers-in-law go far away, thinking I was 34
some kept woman?[11] I did not get up before them
and prepare fine food. Nor did I assemble my
companions to sing songs for them. I could not
perform the customs of our realm. Mother, I am
useless; the Baloch's promise is precious.

35 First you fulfill your promise, then it is up to Punhun to fulfill his. Do not forget the vow you made to the Hôt.

36 The beloved made you thousands of promises, Sasui, but still you will have to press on in order to be true to the name of love.

37 Having heard his promises, Sasui, do not sleep. What can you do to him, if he is untrue to what he said?

38 The sun sets, and Sasui weeps tears of blood. There is no messenger or traveler whom she can ask about his country. Even though she is confused, she does not think of going back.

39 "My feet are blistered, I do not have the strength to walk. Let no woman joke about my going back. My heart has been broken into pieces by the Harho."

40 Her friends talked a lot about going back, but the washergirl[12] planned to get to Punhun on her first attempt.

41 Do not let me die after I have returned, mother, let me die before I turn back. Oh, may I fall on his footprint and writhe in agony for my beloved.

42 When I fled from Bhambhor I searched the hills. I hurried on and reached Kech, where Punhun

himself dwells. You are in everything, so who are those whom you condemn?[13]

When I entered into myself and talked with my soul, 43
there was no mountain in the land and no desire for the Kechis. I myself became Punhun, while I suffered as Sasui.

I myself became Punhun, the veil of Sasui disappeared. 44
The women who set out alone found their good name destroyed. The business they had by the Vindar was accomplished right here.

I myself became Punhun, Sasui's beauty disappeared. 45
He created man in his own image[14] was the talk of the trees. In her desire the mad girl took the Hôt in her embrace.

Sasui's beauty disappeared, she herself became 46
Punhun. Everybody's destination lies there, says Shah. Our connections with Bhambhor[15] block us from the beloved.

I was lost in delusion, otherwise I myself should have 47
become Punhun. I came to the beloved and lost my own identity. Without seeing the beloved, knowledge is not of the least use.

If you once give up your existence, you get near to the 48
beloved. *I saw nothing, all I saw was God.*[16] If you

build your hut beside him, the Hôt will never be far from you.

49 The Hôt is in your embrace, why inquire of travelers? Understand the truth that *He is inside yourselves, do you not see?*[17] No one goes to a shop to look for Punhun.

50 The Hôt is in your embrace, why do you look for a messenger to tell you about him? *We are closer to him than his jugular vein;*[18] thus your beloved is with you. It is your self that blocks you from him.

51 I searched everywhere for my beloved camel man. *God encompasses everything*[19] is the sign of Punhun. He himself is in everything, there is nothing besides the Baloch.

52 He gave this sad creature the cup of separation. The Hôt lit the blazing furnace of love in my heart. The sight of my beloved's hair has taken away my peace.

53 His hair had a violent effect upon me, the pain is not cured by any medicine. Yesterday I saw his beautiful ringlets on his cheeks.

54 She who is slain by his ringlets hardly needs a shroud. She rejoices in her robe of martyrdom.

Oh lord of the mountains, do not overwhelm these helpless creatures. The honor of us all is in your hands, says Latif. Do not say anything, my happy husband, to destroy this helpless creature. Oh you who know everything, for God's sake be content with those who travel on foot. Oh Hôt, do not abandon the one who is wedded to your name. 55

She climbs the mountain with feet softer than silk. The soles of the poor girl's feet are wounded and gashed. Such is the sad state in which she makes her way toward Punhun, saying, "Oh, may he come back, the one to whom this slave girl is bound." 56

Those who would go to the Vindar should gird their loins. Others who intend to give up halfway have no need to start out. 57

His land is far from mine, he is even farther away than distant lands. Sasui has embarked on a long journey to find her beloved. Oh Hôt, you for whom I live have gone to the court of Ari Jam. 58

"We were together, then he got up and went away in the night. Punhun departed after threading my soul with pain. Oh fate, pause a moment so that I may once more be together with him. 59

My soul has no peace at all, my heart is grieved without my beloved. My mighty one has gone, 60 enchaining me with love. My heart and body and all I own are now the property of the Hôt."

61 Those who search for Punhun spend their whole life in love. Why should fickle women strive to imitate them? Great is the fortune of those who die on the way.

62 The beloved is not found by sitting or by sleeping. He comes to those who weep on the paths they travel.

63 The mountain sand has distressed her, but still she climbs on. She searches the mountain paths, says Latif, and goes toward her lord. All Sasui's finery is left upon the sands. Her beloved has brought her suffering, not joy.

64 Look for a clue from within, and search for him in everything, Sasui. Sift through this great heap, and rub the dust on your face. If you follow this advice, you will enjoy a rich reward.

65 If you catch fire, then go on burning. Blow on it until it reaches the sky. Forget all things that exist here. Consign all the world's substance to nonexistence.

66 How will you get to Punhun, you defiant creature? Sasui, the defiant were torn to pieces. You wretched girl, be humble and lose your pride before the Hôt.

The girl has been struck by the arrow of suffering; see 67
how she lies there in pieces. She does not die or live, but dashes herself upon the ground. Sasui is always ready for pain, says Shah.

"I am helpless, without support, weak, and without 68
a guide. I weep tears of blood for my lord, says Latif. I shed tears of longing for my Hôt in the Hab.[20] I will beguile my beloved Punhun with my helplessness. I will grind grain and cook it if you take me with you.

I am helpless, without support, weak, and without a 69
guide. I have been brought to death by my beloved from another country." You are the only support that Sasui has in her distress, says Shah. Oh foolish girl, when you lack any provision, how can you yearn to be with him?

You are helpless, without support, and weak, but 70
become strong and true. Be properly cooked, says Shah, as you roast upon the rocks. Anxieties beset the helpless girl. Through being dyed in the sufferings of her journey, she has become fully colored, says Latif.

Azrael[21] came and wakened Sasui as she slept. She 71
thought that Punhun had sent his man to her.

72 When she saw Munkir and Nakir,[22] she arose before them and asked about Punhun: "Brothers, did my beloved's company pass by this spot?"

73 Keep close to the Kechi and break the stones on the path where his company passed. For your husband's sake, dye the whole of the sand red with your blood. Search the mountain paths, says Latif, get up and explore the mountains. The camel man moves quickly; hasten to catch up with him.

74 Suffer hardship, go into the jungle, and do not hunt for Punhun on the Harho. Pain is your good companion, Sasui, cross the mountain passes with it. Then, oh girl, you may meet the band of your beloved.

75 Woman, cry out, make an effort, do not just sit in Bhambhor. Climb the harsh mountains and look for Punhun's tracks. If you search, you will find a sign of Hôt Punhun.

76 Do not just sit and forget him, inquiring about the way he went. It is those who travel and whose gaze is pure who find him.

77 Unguided in the wilderness, she searched great areas of the country. She traveled without a guide and did not reach her goal.

Oh wind, do not destroy the track I am following. Oh storm, I entrust my beloved's trail over the mountains to you. Do not wipe out the guide I follow in the desert. 78

Do not search far, Sasui, and do not just sit patiently.[23] Give up traveling on foot and forget about sitting. Get rid of any connection with joy, says Shah. Go with your heart, so that your journey may be completed. 79

The steps she took in weariness brought her near to him. With one great effort she managed the whole journey across the Pab. 80

Everyone travels hundreds of leagues, but in your weariness take just one step. Press on in eagerness, so that your journey may soon be completed. 81

Now I will travel alone to Punhun. My path is crossed by mountain passes and lofty peaks. But the pains caused by my beloved are my friends and my companions. 82

She saw the beloved in her heart, and did not get tired or rest. She searched the passes, says Latif, and entered the rocks. Sasui was exalted by the rich treasure of her love. 83

84 "Come near, beloved; do not go far from me, my love. Come back or I will die among the rocks, and it is you who give me life. Oh Hôt Punhun, do not abandon this foot traveler on her journey.

85 Come near, beloved, do not inflict burning pain upon this sufferer. You have gone, Punhun, and abandoned me to the tiger of love.

86 I will never give up patience and gratitude. Oh husband, that time of delight is forgotten.

87 Since my beloved went, I have no peace. Oh God, bring back the one who made me experience desire.

88 Since my beloved went, I have no peace here. My love for Punhun made me experience desire."

89 Become all ears, the Kechis are speaking. Do not say anything, they are talking. What they mean may be heard from their silence. Sit near to them, listen, and acquire passion.

90 "Come, listen and acquire passion," is what they said today. They have learned no other words, all they say is: "Flee from self." Do not make a sound like an instrument; listen and let duality slip away.

The knife and the slaughter are what happen in the 91
courtyard of Ari Jam. The beloved is the blood
money for those who die on the way.

The eyes of Ari Jam are with this blind girl. They guide 92
me to the trees of the Vindar. They see the face of
Punhun and show it to me.

Do not call except for the calls to him, do not travel 93
except for the travel toward him, do not burn
except for the burning for him, do not weep
except for the weeping for him.

Where did it go, that love which always wakes me and 94
woke me yesterday? That careless love went away
after it had roused me, friends. Its turmoil wounds
me, and its pain does not let me sleep.

Now that you are an adult, Sasui, clothe yourself 95
in immodesty. Abandon shame, says Latif, and
wander in the desert like a vagabond. Then your
husband the Hôt will appear before you in his
majesty.

The girl is not one of those who is shaken by the sight 96
of the mountain passes. Sasui has learned the
ways of the foragers.[24]

Do not sit in a grass hut, girl, get up and go on in the 97
heat. You have married a husband whose land is

distant. Enter every area and go around asking for your beloved.

98 Troubles have come to assail this helpless creature.
"Husband, do not dismiss this girl of humble birth from your heart." Forsaking other attachments, go on to your husband and be true.
Dyed in the way, you will become a precious color, says Latif.

99V That beautiful Hôt has departed. I have no power over Punhun's kinsmen.
Sasui searches for the homes and dwelling places of his company.
Did you meet any of Ari's tribesmen going this way?
Their camels were decorated with bells and tassels and ornaments.
He who is the glory of his clan will take me with him.
Sisters, says Abdul Latif, my darling beloved has come.

9 *Ma'zuri*

As they travel toward Hôt Punhun, many false women 1
become exhausted. Rocks become level ground for those who roam in search of the beloved. All friends on this journey of desire are purblind and confused. Oh Brahman girl,[1] turn into bits of meat for the dogs of Kech to feed upon.

She was remembered by the animals Prince Punhun 2
kept. Woman, it was after you died that you got to be with the beloved.

My beloved's dog woke me like a wasp. It barked, got 3
up, shook itself, and glared. With its growling it will remove all this poor creature's pains.

His dog desires dead meat. We are like the flea that 4
clings to Peacock's[2] ear.

Their owners whistle to set them on us, and the dogs 5
bark. They did not disobey the commands they were given, they are as precious as pearls. It is not the dogs' fault; they bark because they have been set upon us.

It is fine if the wild beasts of the mountain attack me. 6
They are no match for the washergirl,[3] they are well aware who her beloved is. They know of her

relationship, says Shah. They might not have held back, but they were affected by her ties to him.

7 Because of my relationship with the mighty one, I have become famous in foreign lands. Otherwise who would the Brahman girl be, and who would she belong to? Sindh would not have heard of her, but now she is famous in many other lands.

8 Sisters, blessed are those who are bare of ornaments and have forgotten their joy. Abandon your laziness, friends, and set out unadorned, all of you.

9 Set out unadorned, all of you, giving up greed and desire. The beloved cannot be gained by sleeping.

10 Set out unadorned, all of you, abandon dressing up. She who takes nothing with her goes in front of all the others.

11 She who took nothing with her reached the beloved. She who wore fine clothes lost the chance to be with him.

12 With vermilion in the parting of her hair and kohl on her eyes, she lost the chance to be with him. She was robbed like Lila, who exchanged her lover for gems.[4]

The Hôt is remote from those tied to existence; he is close to nonexistence. The beloved is gained by those who are loaded with "not."[5] 13

Oh, take the dagger of denial and strike the mule of the lower self. Sell, says Shah, all the baggage of desires. If you step forward with understanding, you will find your journey light. 14

Those who traveled light got across the Harho, so journey alone, girl. The Hôt will never be with those who carry baggage. 15

Those who traveled light got across the Harho, so give up your finery, you wretched girl. Arise and take "not" with you, and be delivered to Kech with nothing. 16

The lovely girl's fate is to be nothing here and nothing there. She did not get there with goods, but reached the Hôt with ecstasy. 17

"On my journey to the Harho I must travel many leagues. Without Ari Jam I have endured cruel sufferings. I have had to travel, says Latif, through many passes large and small. To journey after Punhun is a piece of good luck for me. I have given up everything for him; it is beyond me just to sit here. 18

19 Oh trees, do not grow in my path. Oh mountains, do not rise so high. Do not shed tears, oh my eyes, so that I may see my beloved's track.

20 Oh trees, will you not give me some guidance? Do not let this helpless creature get lost on these twisting paths. Be our guide and let those who travel on foot advance. Get me to my beloved, to avoid getting shriveled up.[6]

21 Thousands of thorns may prick my feet, and they may be so cut to pieces by the rocks that my big toe is separated from the others. But as I make my way toward my beloved, I will not wear any kind of shoe."

22 Shoes are worn by those who love their feet. For the sake of her beloved, Sasui has given up all these conventions.

23 Live as if you were dead, so that you may enjoy the beloved's beauty. If you follow this advice, maybe your existence will be vindicated.

24 Die today before your death[7] in order to be exonerated. So long as you live, woman, keep away from Bhambhor. Be united with Punhun, and rejoice in the angel of death.

Die while you are still alive, Sasui, before the time appointed for your death. Do not shun the company of those who have sacrificed their souls on the path. 25

Those who die before their death never die at all. Those who live before their life in the world to come will live forever. 26

The mountain is high and steep for those who cling to life. Travel with me, oh death, so that I may follow you. 27

Existence, you are attached to many. Life, get into a corner. Death, come to me, so that I may follow you. 28

You did not learn to die for the beloved in secret. Woman, you have not heard of *Die,*[8] so why cut off your head? 29

Go on your hands and feet and knees, and especially go with your heart. Be true to your love of Ari Jam. So long as you live, do not consider anyone to be the equal of Punhun. 30

Go on your hands and feet and knees, and go at headlong speed. Oh woman, remain aware of your love. Let love be your support, Sasui. You may 31 have thousands of Hôts, but do not consider any of them to be the equal of Punhun.

32 Although she is tired, she does not sit in the cool, but strides out in the heat. In the forest, Sasui has become exhausted. On the way, she keeps asking the birds for directions. They take pity on her and tell her about the trees that grow there. Perhaps Punhun may be pleased and return.

33 Whether you stride out or take small steps, the least thing that is written in your fate cannot be lost.

34 The fate written on the forehead can in no way be changed. Whatever the beloved has written on your tablet will assuredly come to pass.

35 For the Kechi she gave her body a roasting. Abandoning all arguments, the poor girl entered the mountains. Though weak and feeble, she pushed herself forward on her journey.

36 "What will people gain from taunting me?" The girl who is filled with love is broken into bits as she follows his trail.

37 She has thrown away tomorrow and drawn on her today.[9] This poor girl's reins are in your hands; in helping her let there be no delay. Either kill this poor wretch or let her come to you.

The wretched girl wants her hopes to be fulfilled, but 38
death has come to stand before her. "If you come, I will perform tomorrow's prostration today. Either take this wretch's existence away or let her come to you."

Suffering and burned, she is scorched by her love for 39
Punhun. Her peerless beloved set her on fire, but he did not burn Sasui completely.

Sasui, have no doubt that for him to see you is far 40
better than your being finely dressed. Be his humble slave, fill his water bags, and do not tremble when you see the mountain pass. A moment with Punhun is wonderful; curses upon twelve years with others.

See, the mountains beat their breasts in mourning for 41
the sad girl. The deer in the desert weep over her death, and as they wander they say, "The dead girl has brought us mortal suffering."

Bitter cries are heard in the mountains over the fate 42
of the sad girl. When the Kechi struck her it was because of some quarrel. The Hôt lies in the lap of those die at his hand.

The trees and vegetation in the mountains utter 43
loud cries over the sad girl. Cut off herself, she wounded those whom she had sat beside.

44 Cut off herself, she wounded those whose blood is never seen. Those who saw the sad girl accepted death.

45 The cut reed utters sad sounds,[10] the slain Sasui loudly laments. The one remembers its green shoots, the other sheds tears for her beloved.

46 Although so many suns have set, I have not been united with my beloved. When it is time for me to go from here, may I see him as I die.

47 I have not been united with my beloved, but my final breath has come. In my death agonies I long for him, in tears I ask the way. May my life not leave me without my seeing my beloved.

48 I have not been united with my beloved, but Azrael has come. Oh my friends, there can be no argument with that mighty one. Death has come to guide me, stopping me from my desire.

49 She strides along and climbs the trees;[11] in tears, she sees the clouds of dust, saying: "How can I move ahead and remove the distance between us?"

50 She strides along and climbs the lofty trees today, and begs them to assist her for the sake of her beloved.

She strides along and climbs the trees, wearing a skirt of silk. Sasui leaps from branch to branch like the young of a peacock. 51

She strides along and climbs the trees—see how strong she is. She stumbles along in the middle of the night, with no mother or father at her side. All she has with her is her voice, which echoes far and wide. 52

A cry arose in the wilderness, like the cry of the *koil*.[12] This cry and this lament were actually both the sigh of love. 53

A cry arose in the wilderness, like the cry of the crane. This cry in the fertile glade was actually the sigh of love. 54

A cry arose in the wilderness, like the sound of the fiddle. People thought it was made by a woman, but it was the sound of love. 55

Oh friend, Abdul Latif's well-being lies in trouble and humiliation. 56V
I am unable to utter praises of what suffering is like.
I spell it out with passion, reading it with love.
The sadness caused by Hôt Punhun is all my joy.
My comfort lies in being starved of my beloved's embrace.

10 Desi

1 "The camels, his brothers, and the mountains, all three have given me grief. But I thought that all of them were joys, because they brought me close to my Hôt.

2 I am smitten by the sorrows brought by the camels, his brothers, and the mountains. I must walk on and trace Punhun's path. This is written in my fate; why else would anyone travel through the desert?

3 On the day you saw strange camels in your courtyard, Sasui, you should have sat till dawn and blocked their exit. You should have used your plaited hair like chains to bind the beasts tight. Then they would not have taken your Hôt away with them.

4 On the day you saw strange camels in your courtyard, if you had somehow hidden the keys to the locks, Sasui, you would have been looked after on the next day.

5 The camels used to make a noise, but when it came to my turn they were silent. When they were being saddled, the wretched creatures said nothing to one another. There was some secret pact between them and their riders.

What if his brothers were against me? If only my fate 6
had not been against me. Is destiny in the hands of camels and camel riders? Who is this poor girl to act against what is ordained?

One should have a lover from one's homeland, what 7
sort of a lover does a stranger make? Having loaded up their goods, they leave for their own land. Now that the beloved has departed, have done with Bhambhor.

Do not bring the camels near me, for I have been 8
grieved by them. Beat the wretched creatures and ride them far away. It is just now that they took Punhun, my Hôt, away with them.

The camel men have all gone off there, but here they 9
remain close to my heart. What pleasure I am given by the movement of those four-toed beasts. The silence of those dumb animals brought me grief and has brought me to these mountains.

May the dust not fly up from the path and fall on my 10
darling. May the fierce sun not strike the camel that carries my beloved. Oh Punhun the pure, my Hôt, you should not be so cruel.

As they departed, the camel men practiced great 11
deceit. The fragrance of Ari Jam comes to me

from every tree. The wild beasts may eat my flesh, but my bones will walk on toward my Hôt.

12 The camels are my enemies, the camel drivers are my enemies, so too are his brothers. My fourth enemy is the wind that has effaced his tracks, the fifth is the sun that set too late, the sixth is the rocky ground that does not let the path run straight, and the seventh is the moon that did not rise in time. I stride through the rocks at the end of the day when the birds come to their nests to rest."

13 Her friends joyfully gathered around the girl, saying: "*Journeying is a piece of hell fire,*[1] turn back, you fool. Ahead you will have to face *the straight path.*[2] Since your love is insincere, how will the Kechi take you with him?"

14 "When *Be and it was*[3] was uttered, Punhun took my soul. From the Day of the Covenant I have been destined to be his. Lord Ali said: *Whoever looks for a thing and makes an effort will find it.*[4] This Tradition is still my support. Because of Punhun's message, death is welcome to me. Pray, my friends, that I may be united with him.

15 Everything is darkness without Ari Jam. Without my beloved I can discern no brightness. Remove the dark smoke from my heart and make it clean, my dearest. *He who has no guide, has Satan for a*

guide;[5] without him there is only gloom. She who travels alone is led astray by pride. *He who travels on the mystic path without a guide* [*is like one who sails on the sea without a boat*],[6] this is not a good saying. Without him, millions have gone astray.

At dawn my companions fill the water bags in their 16
hands. They do not tell me the secret of the camels, says Latif. They are taking away Hôt Punhun, this foolish girl's support."

Today the camel men make haste to leave. His 17
kinsmen take counsel with each other in their private language.[7] Speaking in Balochi, they are taking Hôt Punhun away.

She looks and goes along paths where a five-year-old 18
camel is scared and cannot go, and passes where four-year-olds cannot proceed. Sasui proceeds with great fortitude along ways that are too much for five-year-olds, says Latif, and difficult routes that full-grown beasts find hard.

"Alas, alas," she cries, hitting herself against the 19
stones. Then, says Latif, the girl finds the place of the camel men. Thanks be to you, oh God, that she caught up with them in a pleasant spot.

"For God's sake, you camel men, do not drive the 20
camels so fast. Grab this wretched girl by the hair

and take her with you. See how I suffer on account of my dear Hôt. I will disgrace my family if I turn back this side of Kech.

21 So many wretched women have died near Kech. Twenty paths lead there; how do I know the one they took?

22 A splendid caravan came in fair array from Kech. The camels wore bells and had beautiful aigrettes on their necks. I would call myself Daulat,[8] your humble maidservant, if you took me with you.

23 On their saddlecloths were decorations and thousands of diamonds. The branches of the trees beside the road touched Punhun. Did you meet a company of riders like this as they went by?" "A group did pass by yesterday, woman, but you are looking for them today."

24 "The guests brought their riding camels and made them sit in the campground. Like a sea eagle they snatched him in their claws. The cruel man of the hills destroyed me when he left me while I slept.

25 I thought that my beloved would be with me forever. He was taken on a broad circuit across the plain. I have given my life in exchange for him in the wilderness."

I thought my beloved would be my guest forever. He 26
went away and slew me, not showing the slightest mercy. He gave a load of grief to his maidservant. Last night, dear friends, the camel men did a cruel thing."

Love led her to the desert; otherwise, would a 27
happy woman be filled with longing? In grief she searched fervently in the mountains for his brothers. At last her husband came back to her, and her journey turned out well.[9]

"There was no trickery in my husband, his kinsmen 28
played a great trick. I will go out and search for their camels in the desert. Get out of my way, oh rock that stands before me, lest you break into pieces.

Between us there are many twists and turns, and 29
many mountain passes. What can they do to those women who suffer on their way to the divine beloved?

Alas, the cruel Arichos have taken my husband away. 30
They brought messages from Ari for Punhun. They made plans among themselves, keeping them secret from me. Organizing their company, they fed me false hope. Sisters, the camel men wrought havoc as they departed in the night.

31 Alas, his kinsmen turned against me and took my husband away. Now it is the day of judgment, and all that is promised for doomsday has come true.

32 Alas, his handsome bearded brothers have taken my husband away. For his sake I will jump across the terrible mountains. Which road leads to Kech? I will do my utmost to go there.

33 May he, for God's sake, spend a little time with this sick creature. Whether here or there, I am in the power of Ari Jam. May the pure one drive out my grievous faults. May the perfect one take this washergirl into his care and bring her to Kech.

34 Friends, I suffered when I lived in the quarter of the washermen. They brought me troubles and torment. Now fate has brought me into the company of the travelers."

35 "We are washermen, the servants of Prince Punhun. The Hôt is used to musk; I smell of soap. May none of the girls in the spinning party expose my husband.

36 I am the sort of woman who calls her maid her mistress.[10] Wretched as I am, Punhun became a washerman for my sake."

Together with the washermen, Punhun holds clothes 37
in his hand to wash them. Then there came a messenger from Ari Jam, saying: "Oh perfect one, it is not your task to pound the clothes."

This woman has no kin, either in Kech or in 38
Bhambhor. She alone is anxious; the Hôt is free from care. With the beloved, the only thing that works is humble supplication.

The musk deer intoxicated with its scent and the 39
phoenix in perpetual flight are both distracted in the world—perhaps it is from them that Sasui has learned to suffer.

Last night she saw the white-footed antelopes and 40
thought that the camel men had come. Her love and desire has made her wise. She was quite ignorant, but her sufferings have made Sasui aware.

Those who have no provision with them are supported 41
by the Hôt. Doing a round dance in the hills, Punhun himself will come. In an instant there will be delightful company, says Latif.

Sasui crossed the mountains that confounded heroes. 42
The great peak was leveled flat by love.

43 "I think that the hills Kanbho and Karo are black clouds.[11] Early in the morning I will leave Mount Pab behind me. It is time for me to go, I will not take a break or rest.

44 The mountains and the black clouds merge into each other. The rocks are cruelly hard, full of difficulties and twists and turns. I am weak and helpless as I traverse the ground on foot. You are the helper of this confused creature on these paths that are full of torments.

45 The paths up the mountains are twisting and difficult. In my longing I have cried out to my beloved. Surely my call will reach the ears of the Hôt. All I can do is speak, it is the Baloch's job to listen.

46 The paths up to the mountains are twisting and difficult. Those tribesmen took my husband away with them across the desert. This poor creature's feet are wounded as she climbs the ascents. They have accomplished the plan that was in their hearts."

47 The hills are hard and the journey is long, where mountains and wilderness are seen. The clever forget their cleverness, and experts are amazed. Sasui, says Shah, traversed the plain with love. She who has the son of Ari[12] for her guide is unaccompanied by fear.

The hills are hard and the journey is long, through mountains of many kinds. The camels' cries, says Latif, echo in the narrow defiles. Those who have seen Punhun's footprint do not weep or speak. Those who are alive[13] are attached to the world. 48

The hills are hard and the journey is long, where the camels groan as they go. In her attachment to her beloved, she makes great efforts by the Vindar, saying: "I am left here, come to me, hurry to this wretch." The Ariyani is the support of the helpless. 49

The hills are hard and the journey is long, where the rain pours down. The difficulties of the Harho are renowned, says Shah. In its dark places, oh my protector, make haste to come to me. 50

The gem that gleams in the dark is my dear relative.[14] At the time of reckoning on the day of resurrection, he will not leave me. He will remember me and call me to him, my mountain lord of Kech. 51

"I have become entangled in my love for Punhun, and dwelling in ugly Bhambhor has become deadly for me. Sisters, do not keep advising me to come back. Dear friends, my life is handed over to the care of the Hôt. 52

53 This poor girl has been made to suffer torment upon torment. Her breast has been struck by the arrow of love, so that she keeps company with the wild beasts in the desert.

54 This sad, afflicted girl cannot bear what has befallen her. Oh my Hôt, your servant cannot get there without your help. Come, Ari, I will clutch your hem and get through the pass.

55 If you are ever moved by mercy, my beloved, send me greeting. My longing for you, my dear, has finished off my body. Working with my hands has become deadly for me, and sleep is banned from my eyes. Friend, I cannot endure a single moment while you spend your time by the Vindar."

56 The desert is all fragrance, the mountains have sent forth scent. Bhambhor is filled with delight; every place smells sweet. The faces of the queens are happy, and the sorrows of the maids have disappeared.

57 "Friends, since I became connected by marriage to the Jats,[15] the mountain prince has destroyed my body. Since then I have been half dead.

58 Oh, let no one trust the words of the Baloch. If only I had not slept, friends, and had stayed wrapped in Punhun's embrace. If only the Jats had stayed for

a while in their camp. I am not displeasing to the Kechis, but was unluckily trapped into marriage.

Sisters, I did not behave as one should in love. I did 59
not sleep with my curly-headed lover held tight to my breast. How would the Kechis have driven away with their camels? The fault lies in my fate, let no one speak against Punhun.

Do not forget me, oh my husband, my trust is placed 60
in you. In your kindness, get me across this mountain, which is said to be so dreadful. Arise and come to me soon, Ari Jam. Beloved, let this poor wretch be delivered with your light. Oh pure one, fill this land of darkness with your light. Oh perfect one, hear this poor wretch's cry for help."

Oh my Baloch beloved, do not leave your wretched slave in the rocks. 61V
There is no one like him in the world.
Punhun, take your servant, this washergirl, with you.
I will labor for my beloved and bring him water from the well.
Oh Hôt, do not leave me alone, I have sacrificed myself for the Vindar.
Sisters, says Abdul Latif, the son of Ari will come to me.

11 Kohiyari

1 "You did not awake for an instant *in the night, but slept right through.*[1] *Get up* and reach the beloved, it is not right for you *to sit*. You wretch, sit up all night with your guests. Because you slept at night, you got left behind on the road by day.

2 After *sitting* they got up; the camels uttered a cry. Congratulations to them for being awake, while you were enjoying your sleep. Following the camels, *travel today,* Sasui."

3 Heedless one, abandon your heedlessness. How can you doze, you shameless girl? Silently they set out and got to their journey's end. Get rid of the sleepiness from your eyes, lest you have to cry out in the twisting mountain passes.

4 My eyes became drowsy and sleep overtook this wretched creature. For whom should I now I spend time in this Bhambhor? Sisters, the camel men have hurt my heart.

5 When you slept with legs stretched out, you did something very wrong. If you had only stood by your beloved's door you would have heard them whispering. You are not related by birth to Ari Jam. You were wed to Punhun, but you slept, you wretched girl."

To sleep with legs stretched out is the action of the unworthy. You fool, why do you not search for your Hôt, says Latif? Taunts are directed at the luckless if they sleep. They remained asleep in the evening, so why do they search for Punhun? 6

You slept in the evening, with your face covered like the dead. You did not know how to keep your eyes awake. It was your fault, but you blame the Kechis. 7

"Oh mountain, you are harsh, and so is your behavior. You slice my body like a woodcutter cutting a tree. I am drawn by destiny; why else would anyone travel over the rocks? 8

Oh mountain, if I get to be with my beloved, I will describe the sufferings you have inflicted on me. At dawn you are frightening, and your paths are twisting. You have done me no good in erasing my beloved's tracks. 9

Oh mountain, the first complaint I shall utter to my beloved is this: 'The stones have cut my feet to pieces and pierced my soles. In your heart you had not the least pity on me.' I shall cry: 'The mountain has been very cruel to me.' 10

Oh mountain, you should give cheer to those who are sad. You should take great care of those who have 11 been abandoned by the one they love. Why, oh stone, do you hurt the feet of those who grieve?

12 Oh mountain, the tears on the cheeks of those who grieve do not dry up. They dissolve the stones of the Pab. Hosts of sufferings destroyed me when he abandoned me."

13 In her grief she lamented to the mountain. When they heard her story, the wild animals were grieved.

14 The mountains are the pegs of the earth,[2] the beloved is the one who fixes them. You will never find so patient a lover.

15 The two of them sit weeping together, the grieving girl and the mountain. They say nothing to anyone of the love between them.

16 "Oh rock, by making yourself hot, what will you do to those who grieve? If you are the stones of the Pab, my limbs are made of iron. No one is to blame, it is fate that has dealt with me like this.

17 Oh, many are the friends who seek comfort. Grief has made me familiar with the rocks. The distress Punhun has caused me is my guide on this path.

Now do not leave me here in the rocks, my Hôt. For God's sake, take this woman near your camels. I will be the humble servant of the Arichos. 18

Do not leave me on the rocks, it was my pride that detained me. Come, beloved, to those who have been led astray by their false pride. 19

As I was sleeping, mother, thoughts of the Baloch suddenly made me start. Ah, the arrows of the mountain lord affected every part of me. The impact shook my whole frame, and now this poor wretch cannot live. 20

As I was sleeping, mother, thoughts of the Baloch suddenly made me start. Punhun's arrows are tipped with steel. I seized hold of them, but the metal does not come out, however hard I try. 21

Whatever I am, I am the Baloch's slave girl. In my lowliness, what objection can I raise with Hôt Punhun? I was from the beginning fated to belong to Ari Jam. I am less even than the slippers he wears. How can I forget the Kechi and be content? 22

No matter what, I am the Baloch's slave girl. It is because of my relationship with him that Sasui has become famous. He has severed his ties with me, but I must go to the Hôt. 23

24 There is no sign or sound of the Arichos here, sisters. How can I press on and cross the vast range of the mountains? Perhaps now I will die as I search for the Hôt.

25 I cannot endure Punhun's departure, and it is beyond my power to go to him. Oh God, let this humble creature find the path of the Aricho. I ask you, shepherd,[3] about my beloved. Oh rock, show me where he is. It is my eyes' laziness that has brought such trouble to this woman.

26 Have you encountered the people who destroyed me? Without him, brother, there is no strength in my body. I have been pierced by sharp pains since things became too much for me.

27 I have recognized the one who has destroyed me. Punhun used his eyes to shower me with arrows. This creature has passed beyond the power of doctors and has come under the power of the beloved.

28 Punhun sometimes projects moonlight, sometimes darkness. His path appears before me in many colors. First he plunges me into alum,[4] then he colors me with dye.

Punhun's appearance is pure joy. I think the most frightful day is a happy one because of him. Ari Jam's oppression is sweet to me. 29

Without the beloved, I sit and feed on the pain of separation. Mother, why did I not die before these torments? Sisters, you know nothing of the pains I suffer. 30

Sisters, I have fallen sick since my beloved left. That wise mountain dweller is the one I love; which way did he go? The one in whom Sasui delighted has gone to rest in Kech. 31

If I revealed only a little of my true condition, the wild animals would be struck dumb and the rocks would be split, the trees would be burned and no fresh vegetation would grow. 32

If I spoke openly of my true condition, the wild animals would be struck dumb and the shepherd would be shattered. No rocks would remain in place and the mountains would all be burned up. 33

When I consider myself, I find that I am full of faults. Noble Ari Jam, do not leave. Oh support of the helpless, be my guide on this path. 34

35 Why do my friends mourn for those who are in pain? Their hearts have not been wounded, so their tears are hypocritical. They do not think of my beloved love as they utter their laments.

36 How should I weep for my beloved, when I feel no longing within me? In the passes there are bushes that draw blood, and there are enemies on my path. I have heard how those who are afflicted sizzle on the rocks.

37 How should I weep for my beloved, when I do not know how to be consumed? Inwardly I sigh, as I burn in the sickness of love. The discourse of distress is different among the Baloch."

38 Desolation dwells among those who are consumed by passion. Take your love to the seekers of true reality. Those who cannot see properly see triple, but he is one.

39 Get rid of the others and go toward the one. With your defective vision, you see triple, but he permits no distinction.

40 You are still off track and unaware of the path. Become aware, get on track, and discover the path in your heart.

Do not turn back, girl, when you see the Pab. Do not tremble as you go on, it is a carpet that is spread before Kech. 41

Oh, the Baloches will take me with them if they are merciful. 42V
In my pain they will give me a sign in the name of God.
Do not despair of the mercy of God[5] is what the beloved himself said.
Indeed God forgives all sins,[6] this is a true sign.
Sisters, says Abdul Latif, such is the guide.

12 *Husaini*

1 Do not hang back, it is sunset, go boldly on. The sun is in your face, but do not hesitate. If you go as the sun reddens, you will come to where the beloved is with his company.

2 The sun sets after a delay; she has seen the rocks. Sasui's provision consists of pain, says Shah. With head held high, the poor girl slain by grief enters the Vankar.

3 "As I sat, the sun went down over the mountain passes. How will I track him, when my path lies over stones? My connection is with sorrows, my friends.

4 No one should go with me, friends, a wilderness lies ahead. There is no water, the journey is long, in front of me are nothing but sand and wasteland. Maybe one of you might curse the beloved as they were dying of thirst.

5 On the open ground he has left no tracks, he did not wait nearby. He finally went, leaving his tracks as tokens that he had kept faith with me."

6 Did you hear the sweet sound of his voice, or did you lift your hands in vain? Hundreds and thousands

of Sasuis roam in search of their Hôt beloveds. No child of the Baloch has ever learned pity.

It is partly that the earth is hot, mother, partly that she 7
blazes for her beloved. She presses on and yearns for him, caught between both fires.

“The bonfire of the Baloch blazes over my head. You 8
taunt me because you do not understand the truth of my condition. Come near me, mother, so that I may give you an idea of my suffering.

See how the tears rain like water from the eyes in my 9
head. What I thought was love was really flames from the fire.

If my soul forgets my beloved, it would be a good 10
thing if I were smitten by the hot wind and died like the desert lark.

Do not card a cotton ball for me, mother. Kick the 11
spinning wheel and throw the rolls of yarn in the water. The mountain dweller for whom I spun has gone to Kech.

Curses on the Harho, on the Hôt, and on love. Mother, 12
all that I have got from seeing him is death.

Curses on their language,[1] on the Baloch, and on the 13
whole tribe of camel men. He told me to search, then he went into the rocks.”

14 The hotter the day becomes, the faster she presses on with her journey. The Brahman girl's[2] love for the Baloch began in pre-eternity.

15 So long as you live, keep burning, there is no alternative to burning. Go on through heat and cold, there is no time to sit and rest.

16 Press on through heat and cold, there is no time to sit and rest. Otherwise darkness may fall and you will not find the beloved's track.

17 "As I roamed, I thought of the Baloch. I decided that I will leave Bhambhor, where my heart finds no peace.

18 The delights of Bhambhor separated me from his group. With much suffering I will now search the mountains for him.

19 Sisters, flee Bhambhor and be saved. Many friends have already brought suffering on themselves in this place.

20 Sisters, the smoke of hell arises from this Bhambhor. Find a guide and go forth in good time, Sasui.

21 Friends, I think the wilderness is better than Bhambhor. Otherwise my pain would not have led me to search the mountains.

Friends, I think Bhambhor is better than the 22
wilderness. It was there that my eyes saw the
peerless Ari.

The Bhambhor that did not go after the Hôt is utterly 23
lost. The city completely failed to recognize the
peerless Ari. Those who beheld him with their
hearts enjoyed the beautiful lord.

Bhambhor was bad, Ari made it glorious. The lord 24
of the Harho removed anxiety from the whole
world. The girls learned to print on cloth, making
Punhun their pattern. The peerless one came, the
one who adorned them with sorrows.

My beloved left early because he was ashamed of me. 25
It was in Bhambhor that he came to know about
my caste.[3]

Sisters, if I had been related to the tribe of Ari, the 26
mountain men would certainly have called me
when they departed.

If I was their kinswoman, I should have complained 27
about my brothers-in-law. Out of respect I did not
say a word to them. Mother, my caste is a disgrace
to the people of Kech.

If I had spread my hair as a bed covering, your 28
companions would still have gone. Perhaps the
eyes of the Baloch noticed some fault in me.

29 You did not stay awake with his companions, so why do you weep afterward? It was a bad way to behave for you to sleep while they were setting out.

30 I keep calling out, but his companions do not cry out in answer. The camels make no sound in this wretched woman's courtyard. Such are the miseries that happen in this evil Bhambhor.

31 If I travel, he is far from Kech; if I stay, he is beside me. I wandered lost over the land in fruitless search of Ari Jam.

32 If I travel, he is far from Kech; if I sleep, he holds me close. What sort of a relationship do I have with the Baloch?

33 Their camels passed into Las Bela, crossing over the Manban.[4] The Baloch took my husband Punhun Jam on a journey by force, although they had seemed so friendly in Bhambhor.

34 I think of the rocks as my bedstead and the stones as my mattress. Wherever I spend the night, the wild animals are my friends. My yearning for my beloved has made the rocks my bridal palanquin.

35 From those travelers, mother, I have gained much grief. My acquaintance with those voyagers

happened suddenly upon me. Do not stop me, mother; my beloved went away, wounding my heart.

Why did you get tangled up with a foreigner? Your wits were confused, Sasui, when you made a mountain man your husband. Oh Brahman girl who is lost, did you think that loving the Baloch was a game? 36

My neighbors did not hide my disgrace. They revealed my caste to gain favor with Punhun. That is why the Baloch abandoned me as I lay helpless in sleep. 37

Mother, I have been slain by the sound of Husaini.[5] By day I search in pain for my beloved, at night my wounds fester. I fear that separation may come between us. 38

What happens in separation cannot be experienced in being together. When he came to my room the beloved was parted from me.[6] 39

Come back, oh separation, being together has come between me and my beloved. My festering wounds have been closed by being with him. 40

My hopes have been fulfilled, the Baloch have come to Bhambhor. The sight of Punhun filled me with 41 perfect peace. My griefs were all forgotten, and joys sent me their congratulations."

42 Sufferings showed her the painful route to the beloved. Griefs guided her to joining her Hôt.

43 "I would exchange a hundred joys, I would even exchange my head. If I found love, I would give them all for it.

44 The level of my sorrows has never gone down. Mother, they have flooded so much that the waterwheel is submerged.

45 The Baloch's arrow has struck me, his camels have become highwaymen. May the dew they find difficult not fall upon the camels later. My eyes receive their nourishment from the sight of the foreigners.

46 Perhaps those grieved by love have departed from the land. Now who shall I ask for news of the beloved?

47 Everyone else gets handfuls of sorrows, while I get heaps. I carry loads of them as I wander, but those who would buy them have left.

48 Oh sufferer, tie your belt tight around your sorrows. The way to Kech lies ahead; do not get stuck in the passes and die there.

Griefs are the adornment of joys. Joys without griefs 49
are to be sacrificed. Through these heart's
delights,[7] my beloved came to me."

Those who seek him will always see the beloved. 50
Those who look for him will behold the abode of
the beloved.

If you have asked about him, then press on; otherwise 51
abandon your search for the beloved. Those who
search are never far from the Hôt.

"I search and search, but may I never find the Hôt 52
and be with him, in case the desire in my heart is
diminished by finding him.

I search for you, may I never find you, beloved, may 53
you remain far away. May I never find any comfort
in anything besides you.

I have abandoned my resolve to go forward, having 54
experienced the steepness of the mountains.
Sisters, my heart is entangled with the Hôt.

She who is wedded to the Baloch will find her body up 55
on the scaffold, as she weeps tears of blood.

They have crossed my courtyard and left. Mother, I 56
am dying. I fall in pieces at his feet, crying 'Alas,

alas!' It is not right for me to live, for my beloved has turned away from me.

57 If I had known that I was to suffer the misfortune of separation, I should from the beginning have erased the writing of fate. Then perhaps I should not later have undertaken the labor of traveling to Kech.

58 Light the smoke of pain, woman, and go with them. Do not break the tie of love, for the company is going to climb the mountain passes.

59 Do not become separated from the caravan, for the company is going to climb the mountain passes. Otherwise you will be left behind and be unable to find the way they have gone.

60 If you seek the beloved, turn your back on the practice of abstinence. Those who have seen the Baloch have distanced themselves from all religion.

61 My heart is not cut by any knife, but by distress. I have been killed by agonies that prevent me being restored to life, friends.

62 He inflicted jagged wounds upon my heart. Even though I try to sew them up, it cannot become whole since my beloved left.

Weep, abandon gaiety, and cling to the thought of his 63
caravan. I had only two or three days to be with the Baloch.

I am wretched, and my hut is filled with weeping and 64
wailing. I am slain, and the pain of love is burning in my heart. For the Baloch I will melt the Harho with my blood.

What will you gain by weeping, is your Baloch coming 65
back to you now? Friends, her beloved has done her great wrong. I swear to you that no one should deceive me.

Do not burn this wretch who is already burned up, do 66
not set this miserable creature on fire. For once put out this fire with a shower of water, like the blacksmith does.[8]

If you had died yesterday, you would have joined your 67
beloved then. No case was ever heard of a healthy woman being united with the one she loves.

I will die sooner or later anyway, so it would be good if 68
I died on the way. Then, friends, my blood would afterward be on my beloved's head.

After suffering hardships, die in the Pab for Punhun, 69
so that your friends may all gather and utter your praises."

70 She smiles as she strides along, crying out to him. No glory will be gained by those who turn back before they die.

71 Stride on ahead, do not reveal anything of how you are. Grief is the glory of those who love Punhun.

72 Never give up your cries, let one call succeed another. Perhaps you may thus be remembered on the way.

73 "I have been nourished by sorrows and reared by worries. I was granted no portion of joy, says Shah. Perhaps I was a part of the creeper of sorrow.

74 There are no seekers of divine reality, but reality stands ready for them. I look for them, but there is a shortage of seekers, and they have taken it away with them.

75 What love are you tied up in, to stop you coming back to me who pines for you? Behave toward me while I still live, beloved, as you will after I am dead.

76 Do not be downcast, I am not far away from you. Though it may appear I am far from you, we are actually together."[9]

The camel men did not do what Ari Jam had said. The washergirl left her village in a passion. She offered up her life, and now she sleeps beside his path in the plain. 77

"Oh mountain passes, did the hems of the travelers' garments touch you?" "Mother, he went weeping more tears of blood than you."[10] 78

The foragers said: "Search for him, the way to Kech stretches far ahead." Plunged in thoughts of him, she strode swiftly on. 79

The lord of Kech acted as the pallbearer of Sasui's corpse. The girl had become exhausted by her desire to see her beloved. The son of Ari brought her from the mountain passes, says Latif. The wretched girl was granted a place at his feet.[11] 80

Alas, Punhun is going ahead; let me go forward too. Otherwise the Baloch may say: "The base-born girl was incapable of doing anything." 81

"The base-born can only do bad things. Behave well, my merciful beloved, and come back. 82

I am not related to him, nor am I his kinswoman. I am base-born and unworthy of the Baloch tribe. 83

84 Let news of my caste not reach Kech. Otherwise Punhun may be ashamed of me before his people.

85 If, like me, your eyes had seen the Baloch, you would have told me to search for him, and gone into the mountains yourselves.

86 As you wander, keep crying 'Alas, alas!' in case you forget that 'alas.' Do not shed tears that can be seen, but weep tears of blood within. Patience is a powerful force; may it quickly bring me to my beloved.

87 The silence of the beloved will slay you, do not shed tears of blood. Do not abandon your humble devotion, girl, pride will lose you your Punhun.

88 In death you will stay fixed on whatever you are fixed upon in life. How will those who do not see Punhun here see him in Kech?

89 I alone wander in the wilderness, all the others travel in his company. Anyone who invokes the name of love will suffer misfortune like me.

90 My heart is tied to Punhun with a knot so tangled that I cannot undo it, however hard I try.

91 I asked the experts about the rocks and the path's ups and downs. Those who go alone fall prey to

bandits. Without a guide, this difficult land does not become easy."

There are hundreds and thousands of robbers in the wilderness. Oh you who travel on foot, take a guide with you in the desert. 92

Do not just talk about love, the ways of love are quite different. Do not break your connection with suffering, deal actively with the pain of separation. 93

Those who saw the beloved made him the ornament around their neck. How can others realize the worth of his alchemy? 94

"Foolish girl, do not let your heart waver; you will experience joy, Sasui. The mountain man is coming to you in joy, leading a train of camels." 95

It was the lady[12] who first mourned in Husaini for Husain. Afterward the world came to learn about it. 96

Oh my Hôt, I will give my flesh to the wild beasts after tearing my body to pieces. 97V
I have set fire to Bhambhor and have come to you.
I cannot manage without Ari Punhun, friends.
In my grief, I put a grindstone on my heart and grind my griefs.
Draw near, my beloved, and do not go far away.

I have seen him; believe me, the vexations of the
journey do not turn me back.
Show yourself to this grieving girl, who dies without
seeing your face.
My beloved's cup, which he has made sweet, has
intoxicated me.
The fire of love for Ari Punhun burns within me.
If I am laid beneath the earth, still I will not leave you.
I will hurl my body into the dust, after severing my
head.
See how this grieving creature is broken on hearing of
Punhun's departure.
Beloved, cast your eyes that are full of kindness upon
me.
Sisters, says Abdul Latif, may my beloved show mercy
to me.

13 *Lila Chanesar*

"The pain you inflicted makes your helpless lovers 1
suffer forever. For God's sake, beloved, do not
go far away. In your presence I am throwing the
jewels into the blazing fire.

I am throwing the jewels into the blazing fire, and 2
putting the necklace in the flames." Shah says: Oh
beautiful woman, how can you rest at ease? The
king is a mighty ruler and very jealous. The lands
that lie in every direction are in awe of Prince
Chanesar. You exchanged for the jewels the lord
who is the delight of your eyes."

Chanesar is twice as hard to grasp as the rest of the 3
world.[1] You broke your ties with him, so that you
might feel the jewels in your hand.

Beguiled by the jewels, you foolishly thought much of 4
yourself. With your words you separated yourself
from Prince Chanesar. The page has turned, and
you have experienced the burning pain of being
rejected.

"The glitter of the gems turned my head. I thought I 5
would win the necklace as a bet, and that it would
be mine forever. Kaunru's trickery beat me."

The gems you saw and were beguiled by are not 6
precious. In fact, they were always beads of glass.

Cursed be the gems that have separated many from those they love.

7 What you thought was a necklace was a string of sorrows. Chanesar withdrew his affections and turned to the maidservant. May no husband behave with such hostility to anyone.

8 “I wore nothing on my wrists and nothing around my neck. I had no decoration in my hair parting or makeup around my eyes, nor any other adornment. It was because I was unadorned that my husband chose me.

9 I wore golden earrings in my ears, deep-colored necklaces around my throat, and bracelets around my wrists, and my hair was oiled and parted with vermilion. That is why my beloved husband ceased to think of me.

10 Look, he was already angry with me, the necklace was a pretext. Friends, listen to me, all of you, my husband is not in anyone’s power. At the very first chance he crushes any attempt to control him.

11 I saw that the groom’s feet were crooked at the time of the covering.[2] I realized at the time that he would treat his bride badly.

Kaunru sleeps in the same quilts, occupying that fair 12
abode. Oh Chanesar my husband, I did not think this of you.

When Lila saw the treasure, she slipped into selfish 13
thoughts. People kept coming and condemning her. With their taunts, they have burned her inside to a crisp. The poor woman has forgotten the high spirits of her childhood.

Were you so clever then, and did you know about 14
your husband? Did you think you would be beautiful with the necklace around your neck? A husband does not like a false wife, no matter how many ornaments she wears. Chanesar is a skilled appraiser who discovers secret thoughts and examines hearts.

"I was the leading lady, my friends gathered at my 15
house. When my hand touched the necklace, I became unpleasing to my husband. My beloved pushed me away, and I suffered the bitter pain of rejection.

I was the leading lady in Chanesar's kingdom. Drums 16
and tabors and pipes would welcome me. My beloved pushed me away; I became disgraced in the land as a rejected woman.

17 I was the leading lady in Chanesar's kingdom. I was greeted in the inner apartments by maids, slaves, and attendants. I was seated in the midst of the company with drums and tabors and pipes. I was my darling's beloved, but then the necklace made me of no account. After that I was disgraced in the eyes of my husband.

18 When I sat on swings[3] I had no awareness. The business of the jewel made me ugly and brought disgrace upon me. Sorrows came to confront me, my husband turned away from me.

19 Lila, mind you do not make yourself conspicuous by talking to Chanesar. You brought ruin upon yourself, you foolish woman, when you quarreled with your husband. You fool, you acted with pride and brought upon yourself the pain of being rejected.

20 Lila, you cannot match up to him by talking to Chanesar. The one you thought was your own is a king jealous of his honor. Love for anyone else does not please your husband.

21 Do not reveal yourself, Lila, by talking to Prince Chanesar. Your beloved Dasaro is exceedingly patient. Your beloved is your protection, a cover over your faults.

Do not reveal yourself, Lila, by talking to Prince 22
Chanesar. This husband does not belong to anyone, not to me and not to you. I have seen many of his darlings weeping at his door.

Oh lovely Lila, give up the clever ways you have 23
learned. Wrap the hem of your garment humbly around your neck and embrace poverty. He will never tell you to go away if you entreat him with humility.

No woman should play the coquette with Chanesar. I 24
realized afterward that this was not the place for flirting. In his fury he swiftly sentenced his happy brides to rejection.

No woman should be flirtatious with Chanesar. The 25
groom does not like pride or arrogance in anyone. If he turns away from them over a small thing, he causes suffering to those who love him.

They were all happily married women, and they all 26
had their faces decorated. Each of them thought that the king would come to her. He entered by the door of the one who was ashamed to look at herself.

Dasaro, I have come to your door after committing 27
countless faults. If there are things that make you

angry in your heart, my husband, then I have no place of support. For the sake of the lord, remove my defects, oh you who conceal all faults.

28 If my awareness is inadequate, then you must recognize who you are. From the beginning you have concealed the faults of the lost to an extraordinary degree. Your glory is such, oh beloved husband, that you cover their faults.

29 You have thousands of beautiful partners, you are the partner of thousands. Dasaro, do not leave me, so that I may not be disgraced. You, Chanesar, are the one who holds the hem of the shawl that is humbly wrapped around my neck."

30V Come, beloved, enter my house, Lord Chanesar. I have given up the necklace.
Asking for Lila and devising their plans, the pair of them[4] came from outside.
Winning my husband's trust, she found a place in the palace.
I am full of defects, faults, and vices. Beloved, overlook them all.
Coming to your door, Dasaro, what displays of love can I make?
I have come, beloved, says Abdul Latif, and entered your door.

14 *Mumal Rano*

Yesterday we met a yogi,[1] a wandering beggar. The 1
master had a ring of cloth on his head and a fine
necklace around his neck. Our heart was wounded
by the fakir when he appeared before us.

Yesterday we met a yogi, shining like the moon. The 2
fakir aroused passion and pain in us.[2]

Yesterday we met a yogi, one watch after sunrise. See 3
the beauty of the master, who wept tears of blood,
saying: "Once he has seen Mumal's face, it is hard
for anyone to return."

Yesterday we met a yogi whose body was covered with 4
clay. Wearing a green shawl around his shoulders,
the master had a necklace of gold. "Tell us truly,"
we asked him, "something of Mumal's beauty."

The ascetic went into the desert in a state of ecstasy. 5
Great tears fell from him as he spoke of Kak.
There was something fixed in his body that
opened up wounds that had closed.

The yogi's face was filled with a light like that of the 6
sun at dawn. A fragrance like that of attar came
from his forehead. The ascetic showed us the
place where he had been dyed red.

7 The yogi was completely covered with the jewelry of love. The sunlike master seemed like a moth. He had come from the landing place of Kak, dyed red by the princesses.

8 "Come, dear yogi who wears a loincloth, how did you see the Gujar girls? Your eyes shed tears of blood. Why do you not tell us, master, about the beauty you beheld?"

9 "There are steel axes in the pupils of the Gujar's eyes. With them she deals princes heavy blows. Go and see the foreigners' graves on the banks by Kak.

10 The Gujar comes and stands confronting the yogis who charm snakes. She faces those who fire their arrows on target.

11 Wanton Mumal slays the hunting princes. She has made many learned pandits and *pīrs* tremble. She shoots her arrows at those who wear royal diadems on their foreheads."

12 The yogi aroused us and plunged us into suffering, saying: "There is untold passion on the banks of the Ludano. Go there quickly and see the canals of love.

13 Come, go to the landing places of Kak, where love wells up. There is no let or hindrance, everyone may see the beloved.

Come, go to the landing places of Kak, where love 14
is fashioned. There is no day or night there, everyone may see the beloved.

Come, go to the landing places of Kak, where love's 15
cauldrons boil. Millions are dyed as red as betel juice with love for Mumal.

There are walnuts, grapes, fine sandal trees, and lotus 16
flowers there. The camel enjoyed the garden where no bees buzz about. Let us go there quickly and see the princesses and lotuses of Kak."

The four friends, the Sodho huntsmen,[3] all mounted 17
their camels. The Sodho prince cleverly threw down a betel nut.[4] They rode swiftly on toward Kak, where lovely Mumal lives. The hunters did not return, trampling the lotuses of Kak.

The dresses they wore were like the petals of the 18
rose. Ah, their braided hair is always perfumed with jasmine oil. The sight of their beauty, says Shah, provokes stabbing pains of love. Their lovely appearance stops anything being said in the spinning party.

The green shawls they wore were like betel leaves. 19
They had made their bodies fresh with attar and ambergris. Their braided hair was impregnated with musk and sandal. The lovely woman's ears were decorated with silver and gold. She was

wonderfully dressed and adorned, says Latif. She was happy in heart, thinking: "I am married to the Sodho."

20 The golden-colored Sodho women play with silver. Incense sticks burn in their reception rooms; their divans are scented with musk. Ewers of perfumed water are poured out in their bathrooms. Their traveling lovers are lined up and consumed by the sight of their beauty. To see them, says Latif, they have become ascetics. The yogis come to Kak, dyed red by love.

21 The Gujar girl has wounded many; now she is wounded herself. The arrow fired by Mendhiro has struck her in the head.

22 No one is as beautiful in appearance as Rano, the Sodho is fairer than all. He has removed the black deposit from everyone's heart, says Latif. There is no idea of anyone else, everyone has become Mendhiro.

23 Kak did not detain the ascetics, its palaces did not beguile them. They were not trapped by the snares of the ladies or their maidservants. The yogis paid no attention to the lovely women.

24 Kak did not detain the ascetics, its riches did not beguile them. Being in a lofty spiritual state, they caused suffering to the lovely women. The girls

frolicked about, but the ascetics passed by their charms.

"I burned a candle through the night, until the rays 25
of dawn appeared. For God's sake come back, Mendhiro Rano, I am dying. In search of you I have flown many crows from Kak.

As I stood I saw the stars rise; they have all now set. 26
All night long I thought of Mendhiro and his camel. Tears poured down my cheeks when the sun put forth its rays.

The Pleiades have set, the triple stars of Orion have 27
risen. Rano has not come tonight; the time that he was due has passed. Curses on this wretched night, which I have spent without my love. Inflicting grief upon me, my groom has gone to stay in the Dhat.

Rano went at night, leaving some secret hint. Without 28
the Sodho, friends, I cannot live at peace. I am hopeful, though, that having gone he may return.

The Sodho talked to me while the world slept. If it was 29
revealed, friends, none of you would sleep.

Rano, I watch your path every day. Within my soul lie 30
threads of Rano's sweet talk. I am bound to you, beloved, by nails of love.

31 Rano, my comfort, come, oh lord of food and the earth. Happy brides desire your company, oh Sodho. Oh perfect lord of Kak, do not remove your hand from me.

32 When you have formed a relationship with a man who is noble as a lion, never turn your back on him. Pursue Rano keenly with love. Do not shower your favors on everyone, like the pouring rain. You will think a great deal about the Sodho on the day of resurrection.

33 The same earth that lies under my feet lies above many beloveds. We have stood and seen mighty ones covered in the dust. Everyone is given only a couple of days, get up and search for him, says Latif.

34 You thought Rano was a joke, you went and gave pleasure to some base wretch. Your husband was angry with you, thinking a stranger had come into your embrace.[5] Alas, you broke your compact; you will think a great deal about the Sodho.

35 Kak is consumed, the trees have gone, my heart burns. He slipped off leaving his staff behind,[6] this is the thought that has struck me. Now I cannot live at all; come back quickly, beloved.

36 Kak is consumed, the trees have gone, and the red-painted palace is burned down. Now you

have left, beloved, my heart is overwhelmed with terrors. Oh my beloved, fulfill quickly the promises you made to me.

My being and my property are sacrificed to you, I sacrifice the Ludano. May Rano not be angry with this poor creature who is devoted to him. It is not right to put on airs with the dead, oh Mendhiro. 37

I have no children, no partner, no in-laws, no kinsfolk. Since you left, beloved, I have been overcome by grief. Traveler, give this message to my beloved from the Dhat. 38

Oh my Sodho, wise beloved, turn your camel back toward this poor creature. What do I care for Kak? It is to you that my being is drawn. Abandon your suspicions and go to the courtyard of the one who desires you. 39

Be happy with me, my love, and come to the courtyard of the one who desires you. I cannot bear a moment without you, who make me come alive. Strike me with the spears of love and remove my sufferings. 40

Look at my bedclothes, bolsters, and pillows. My heart burned when I saw the bedding that had been slept in by my beloved. I have to face not only the displeasure of my family but also Mendhiro's failure to return. 41

42 Oh Sodho, my grief has dried up my eyes, which no longer water. They are dry with longing for Rano's company. How can they feel full, Mendhiro, when you have crucified them?

43 If you come to my house, Mendhiro, and be my guest, I will bring my ego and thrust it into the flames. I will thrust my selfhood into the oven and destroy it. Oh Sodho, I will sacrifice my family and my household to my beloved.

44 Pitch your tent in Kak, Rano, and stay here. Check on the men of the palace.[7] Otherwise you are sorry, my husband, you may be sorry when it is too late to do anything.

45 Beloved, do not go to the Dhat, leaving this miserable woman in Kak. I am bound by the promise I gave you in the beginning. Thinking of you, my love, I have wept in my red-painted palace. Believe me, its buildings and its furnishings have become like poison to me.

46 The Sodho took my head, my empty skeleton remains here. My soul is longing for Rano's company. With my eyes I see no one besides you.

47 Friends, Rano has treated my heart cruelly. Mendhiro has cut my heart, and my body trembles. I think my heart has gone off, and cannot stay in one spot.

Rano, I weep when I see the bedding and the rooms. 48
Dust gathers on the beds and the bedsteads are
in disrepair. The pillows placed upon them have
become covered with dust without my husband.
The buildings, flowers, perfumes, and trees have
all faded without you. Oh Mendhiro, who besides
you can I put on airs with?

You were very cruel, Mendhiro, when you came 49
and then went back. Were you not my partner,
husband, if only you had stayed and woke me up.
Then, oh Sodho, you would quickly have become
aware of who it was that slept.

The Sodho has not learned to speak out like the rest of 50
the world. Rano does not shed heavy tears down
his cheeks.

I have had enough of the gardens that bloom on the 51
banks of the Kak. Without my Sodho, friends, I
get no pleasure from the Kak. Rano has cast his
rope and tied my body like a boat.

I did not realize, my love, and I made many grievous 52
errors. Yesterday, oh Sodho, they came back to me.

If only I had realized that your silence was a message 53
for Mumal. Your patience, Mendhiro, was the
right path for me.

54 My beloved covered me, otherwise I was naked. Having given me some protection, he made the Kak my cloud.

55 Oh Sodho, your forbearance gives pride to those who should be ashamed. Those who speak through their silence command respect.

56 Oh Sodho, thousands are taught by your forbearance. My destiny once guided me, but then it led me to a fall.

57 Oh Sodho, your forbearance brings the foolish back. The instrument of patience made me repent quickly.

58 What does it matter to the shameless, who have whole kilns of noses on their faces,[8] if one nose is cut? Those who keep their honor, however wretched they may be, retain their beauty even in their destitution.

59 From Rano's company there came a yogi. The master shed a light like that of the full moon. Darkness was removed by the yogi's light.

60 From Rano's company a yogi came. The whole land was made fragrant by the scent of musk. It was from there that the perfect master came.

A new message came from Rano last night. We received, says Latif, a gift from the bounteous one. Why ask about caste or tribe? Anyone who has come is acceptable. 61

In which direction should I drive my camel? All around there is light. The reddish Kak is within, the Ludano is within. There is Rano and Rano, there is no one else besides Rano. 62

In which direction should I drive my camel? All around there is light. The reddish Kak is within, verdant gardens are within. There is no other sound, it is entirely Rano." 63

Ranas, Rajputs, and Mumals will clearly see. 64V
The learned, pundits and *pīrs*, even lords and Hamirs[9] will die.
Obeying the will of the lord, all will depart from this place.
They will leave, oh guide, according to the word.
He makes the agonies of death easy at the time of farewell.
Oh Ahmad, come there at the time of difficulty.
In the future do no leave this beggar, oh guide.
It is truly said that *All living creatures must taste death.*[10]
Whatever is written in one's fate will assuredly come to pass.
Sisters, Abdul Latif says that the supreme lord will show his grace.

15 Marui

1 "When *Am I not your lord?* fell on my ears, then and there I said with my heart, *They said 'Yes.'*[1] At that time I made a promise to my tribespeople.

2 My heart has been given to the Marus ever since the time of *Be and it was.*[2] Oh Sumiro, why did you put my body in chains? Lord Hamir has acted cruelly in chaining my body.

3 There was no *Be and it was,* the moon had not yet been formed. There was no awareness of virtue, there was no connection with sin. There was oneness alone, there was nothing but divine unity. There, says Latif, she understood a complex mystery. Beloved, with my eyes and my heart I have recognized you.

4 I am confined in *the prison of water;*[3] here I suffer difficulties. *My body is here and my heart is with you*[4]—that is where my heart is. May the almighty reunite me with the Marus.

5 There is no captivity like *the prison of water. The pen dried after writing what was to happen,*[5] and no alteration to that is possible. Umar, may your hands grant freedom to the shepherds.[6]

Without the Bedouin I have to suffer troubles here. 6
Both eyes shed blood in my love for you,[7] may I keep
faith with this love to the end. My heart, eyes, and
body are there, where my friends were born.

Without my countrymen, sisters, I will now burn this 7
place entirely. *All things will return to their origin;*[8]
I pine for the nomads. I would return to my native
place and see the land of Malir.

No messenger from there has reached me. No one at 8
all has come to me, traveling from my brethren.
Who will bring me letters from them?

Oh camel rider, if now you bring me a fellow villager 9
from that land, the foul streets of the fort are
made fragrant. Come, let me use my eyes to wipe
your feet that have traveled in the desert. For
God's sake, says Latif, do not delay. Who can live
in these rooms? My heart is melancholy in the
palace.

How can I write letters that fate seizes and rips in 10
half? Those tied to love are sacrificed on a pyre.
I weep night and day, for in his words there are
many mysteries.

Oh Umar, the Marus have many resting places in the 11
deserts. They have removed the red lac[9] from

their shawls, says Latif. Umar, give the order for me to become a herder and to graze the camels on leaves.

12 There are thousands of patches on my blouse, and my shawl is in rags. Relying on being with my kinsfolk, I wore nothing that they had woven. Oh pardoner of faults, cover me with the shawl I wore in the Dhat.

13 There are thousands of patches on my blouse, and my shawl is nothing but rags. I do not perfume and braid my hair, and let its bunches stay tangled. My heart desires only to see the Maru's face. In this state, oh Hamir, may I return to my homeland thickets.

14 Sewing patches on her dress, the poor girl does not let her love grow less. She darns the edges of her shawl, lest someone should say to her that she has disgraced the women of the Thar.

15 The nomad women of the desert never put on clothes of silk. Their blankets dyed with lac are more beautiful than shawls. Their cloth woven from wool is better than silk and brocade. Oh Sumiro, I consider the cloth they have woven to be superior to scarlet shawls. I should die of shame if I took off the clothes that had been given to me by my family.

I will never wear fine silk clothes. I do not want shawls embroidered with flowers or made of brocade or sky-blue cloth. May I enjoy shawls as white as milk with the Maru. I thirst in my heart for my beloved shepherd nomad. 16

The Maru's betrothal threads are like gold to me. Oh Umar, do not offer silken clothes to this nomad girl. Blessed is the thread of the blanket that my kinsfolk gave to me. 17

The betrothal threads are like gold, every thread is worth hundreds of thousands. For someone who has rejected silver, crores of rupees are like straw. I use the Maru's betrothal oil on my hair, I have no use for yours. 18

I will not use your oil, I have the Maru's oil in my heart. I listen to nothing else, trusting in him alone. 19

The Maru women wear glass bangles on their wrists, taking pride in what most people are ashamed of. 20

We wear black threads around our wrists; for us, gold is a cause of mourning. Blessed is hunger with my friends, I consider starving a delight. 21

It is not the way of the Marus to exchange their kinsmen for gold. Now that I have come to 22

Umarkot, I will do nothing wrong. I will not change the huts that I love for a palace.

23 Blessed are the women of my homeland, whose honor is guarded by the desert. Gum trees and desert creepers are my kinsfolk's covering. In their thickets, the nomads roam covered in creepers. The Marus gave me the wilderness as my dowry.

24 Rainwater is their drink and wool their dress; their feet tread that pure ground. They sit below clumps of trees, that is their safe abode. Those poor creatures are fearless and have no regard for themselves. Oh Umar, they suffer but are not disobedient, do not give them grief.

25 Oh Umar Sumiro, what is Eid for you is a time of mourning for us. The sad creatures have forgotten joy and the pleasures of buying things.[10] The Marus of Malir have been martyred by their desire to see me.

26 Marui does not wash her braided hair, and thinks in her heart of the desert nomads. She who belongs there sheds tears here and makes the land of the Marus weep. She remembers the edge of the desert and is overcome by grief. The lovely woman hears nothing but her nomad tribe. Oh Sumiro, behave honorably and release her from the fort."

I have seen Marui miserable in the palace, with a sad 27
look on her face. She does not oil her dry hair,
and her sufferings have destroyed her beauty.
She is chained in iron, says Latif, her joys have
evaporated like camphor. Those whose hearts are
distressed take no pride in oiling their hair.

Turning her face toward Malir, she weeps and says: 28
"Oh Sumiro, I think your comforts are torments.
I belong to the Maru, I will not be made your wife
by force. My heart is captive to that people, and it
cannot be contained in the fort.

The other prisoners are at peace, I am restless in my 29
chains. The Marus fill my thoughts and hang over
my head like a sword.

Those for whom I wear rags in this world have not 30
asked about me even for a moment. These
windows have broken my heart, and these rooms
have slain me. I am consumed by thoughts of the
Marus; otherwise these mansions do not hurt me
at all.

If I get to be with my husband, then my fortune is fair. 31
Seeing the desert nomads is a fresh experience for
me every day.

Oh Sumiro, how can I stop thinking about the desert 32
nomads? They have been nailed in my heart

without a blacksmith. There are thousands of nails of love for them in my heart. It has been many days since I saw the nomads or their huts.

33 I have destroyed my looks, oh Sumiro, the Marus will hardly accept me. Some of my family have taunted me, others taunt me now. If you remove my chains, I will not remain in the fort.

34 I have destroyed my looks, oh Sumiro, and my face is unclean. I must go to the place where none but the beautiful may go.

35 I have destroyed my looks, oh Sumiro, how will I be accepted? With this ugly face I will be unable to experience married bliss with the Maru.

36 Fair are the faces of the Marus who live in Malir. Their good fortune has favored many who are full of faults. Ill fortune was my fate, so my beauty was spoiled.

37 There is no one besides God the almighty, it is from him that ill fortune comes. *Say, nothing will happen to us except what God has decreed.*[11] This is the place of forgiveness. For Marui good and bad luck are the same.

38 If I went to them in the same state that I came in, the skies would rain with happiness. I must suffer the reproach of this mansion for the rest of my life.

I was disgraced in the eyes of my husband when I came here. How will I hold my head high in the huts of the Marus?

Either I should never have been born, or once born 39
I should have died. Once I was born, I became a source of distress to the Marus.

Lord Sumiro, do not try to persuade me to break my 40
chastity. I will go there in a few days, oh Hamir. Otherwise I shall not hold my head high in Malir.

If only Marui had not been born, if only she had died 41
instead! By coming to Umarkot she has brought disgrace upon herself. She who is entranced with the Marus can take no pride in palaces.

God, may it not happen that I die in captivity. With 42
my body in chains, I weep night and day. Let me first go to my home country; it is fine if my days then come to an end.

For what crime am I made a prisoner? For what reason 43
am I taunted and made to wear chains around my neck? If I die in this place, take my body to Malir.

If I die thinking about the homeland I long for, do not 44
imprison my body in captivity. Do not keep this exile apart from her beloved. Pour the cool earth of the desert over her dead body. Once my life is over, take my corpse to Malir.

45 If I die thinking about the homeland I long for, then take this head to my native land, sir. May I be buried in the desert with the Marus who live there. I will be restored to life after death if my body gets to Malir.

46 If I die here longing for my homeland, oh Sumiro, make my grave with the desert nomads. Let me smell the fragrance of the creepers of my ancestral land. I will be restored to life after death if my corpse goes to Malir.

47 Around my neck are collars of iron, I wear fetters and chains. There are shackles on my feet, and the room is nailed on the inside. There are lookouts in the courtyard, and the ministers are on guard. I am unhappy in my cell; this is the state of my body. Oh Maru, Prince of Malir, ask after this desert nomad.

48 Iron fetters and chains have destroyed me. The anxiety caused by Sumiro left no flesh on my frame. Friends, pray that the honor of my woolen shawl may be preserved.

49 May the honor of my shawl made from white wool be preserved. If it gets holes in it, I will sit and darn them. Oh Umar, let this poor heedless creature be kept safe. I promised my friends that I would be with them in the rainy season.

The desert nomads are smiling, the southwest wind 50
has returned. I have remembered my beloved,
says Shah, his cattle tracks and pens. The
beautiful huts of my husband will be there beside
the dunes.

The desert nomads smile, the southwest winds have 51
brought rain. Their cares have been removed, says
Latif, and their calves walk strongly. Oh friends,
they shear the soft wool from the sheep's tails.
Oh Umar, free from sorrows they spin the wool at
their husbands' side. In the desert even the young
sucklings give wool from their backs. Precious
shawls of high value are woven. As they starch the
shawls, the women say: 'Marui is needed in Malir.'

Every day, oh Sumiro, they gather and cook food from 52
the jungle. They pile up heaps of dried grass, says
Shah. From the *lanb* grass, says Latif, they extract
grains of rice to cook. Oh Umar, they do not
consider pulao to be as good as their *ārāṛī*.[12]

Living in the wild, those happy people are always 53
content with what they find. They bring branches
of berries they have picked and put them on to
cook. The foragers who frequent the thickets are
not thin or weak.

Content with little food, they remain strong and 54
healthy. This is how they go about, in shawls

covered with dust. Go to Malir and discover the honor of the nomads.

55 In their country there is no check or hindrance, nor any revenue tax. They break off the red flowers and throw them in the trough. The Marus are without price and their Malir is a happy land.

56 Carrying baskets large and small on their heads, they are covered in perspiration. Their heels are covered in dust and there is sweat on their feet. This is the way of the desert dwellers, I recognize them by the way they move."

57 Umar tells her: "Here are doors and gates and windows. I will have thousands of tents put up for you. Marui, do not weep and wail for those who have never come to see you." "Those nomads who live on flowers of thorn must be in some trouble," she replies.

58 "My life is sewn to Maru with a fine needle. I sit and think of the creepers and grasses. My heart is there, my body and my flesh are here. My life is in those huts, my frame is in this palace.

59 My heart is sewn to the Maru with a fine needle. My body is now covered with patches of humility. How can my ears be pierced to take your ornaments without my people's needle?

Friends, I do not think kingship can be compared with 60
the needle that covers the naked but itself is bare.
Be born again if you would know the worth of the
needle.

He moves and is ever present in my mind; I cannot 61
forget him however hard I try, ever since the
primal covenant of *Am I not*[13] or even before that.
He does not beget nor is he begotten,[14] what can
Marui do? Whether she dies today or tomorrow,
she will remember her protector.

He moves and is ever present in my mind. I cannot 62
forget him however hard I try. He has given me a
drink from the pool of love. She lives for the huts
of the happy desert dwellers, who come out of
their dwelling places in the rainy season, leaving
their possessions behind.

He moves and is ever present in my mind; I cannot 63
forget him however hard I try. *There is nothing like
him,*[15] but I cannot see my beloved, the nomad
who has built his huts in the land of nonexistence.

They move and are ever present in my mind, they 64
remain in my soul. The Marus go out in the rainy
season, turning toward the borderlands between
the river and the desert. How often I remember
the times that they would churn their pots at
dawn. How wonderful those brackish wells of my
native land were, from which I used to draw water.

65 They dig wells in the desert and water their goats. At dawn the women draw water from wells sixty fathoms deep. Pouring the water into buckets, they cry out with joy. Every day I feel a fresh pang of separation from those who dwell in the desert.

66 The women get up at midnight because the water lies deep in the ground. The heedless ones get no opportunity during the day.[16] It was my bad luck that they snatched me from the well.[17]

67 My friends stopped drawing water, my chaste companions heard what had happened. There has never been a Maru girl in a palace. Oh Umar, if only I had died before I heard their taunts.

68 The ones who go to the well at dawn do not make a sound. The women who draw water have gone to the jungle to sleep beside their mates. On both sides of the well the ropes dangle idly.

69 Oh Umar, everyone is busy, who can I share my pain with? The foragers whose talk I once enjoyed are far away from here. The herdsmen have taken away their huts from the wells.

70 They set up their huts where the rain falls. They have not the slightest awareness of how I am. Perhaps I have been forgotten by the Marus, now that they are content with the food they have.

The rain has fallen on the Marus, yielding fresh grass, bog, and mud. My heart dies thirsting, and my life is consumed longing for them. If only I could drink my fill there. Even a mouthful with the beloved is wonderful, but I care nothing for large cupfuls here. 71

In the dunes of the Dhat the Marus have put up many huts. The whole desert is flourishing, who would stay at home? I am chained in the fort, and my heart is distressed in the palace. 72

In this season the Marus are happy and drive their flocks back to the thickets. They drive the kids to the lower pastures, grazing them on the plains. My eyes shed copious tears over them. The *tāro* birds[18] cry: 'The rains are falling, come back.' 73

In this season the Marus are happy, and are at ease in the desert. The women gather plenty of different grasses and creepers. Do any in the land, says Shah, remember me, their chaste companion?" Latif says: "Do not take off your blanket, my dear. God will be kind to you. The rains are falling, come back." 74

In this season the Marus are happy, they live near the hedges of thorn. There is abundant water in the plains, and they drink it beside their huts. Here she is in chains, says Latif, while they are happy in 75 the desert. People are feeding on the wild fruits of the desert; the rains are falling, come back.

76 It is their mark that they travel with their huts and baggage. They are the noble Marus who traverse the desert.

77 "I would lie down on the goats' droppings with my head resting on my arms. My two eyes and my nose are all streaming as I think of that waterless place. My fellow tribesmen are far away in the desert.

78 Those happy gatherings in the desert, and the wild fruits of the place—when I remember these things, my eyes overflow with tears. My heart is torn by my separation from those I have not seen for so long.

79 I pine and fret, for they are out of sight. God, bring me a camel rider to give me some good news, and remove the ache for my homeland from my heart.

80 Now that it has rained, there is gladness, and happy congratulations are exchanged. All the cares of the women who wear shawls are removed. The Sumiro himself has sent the nomads a message of peace. Now, Marui, you will be honored by the prince."

A camel rider has come from there with accurate news. "Do not forget your husband, woman, and do not grieve. You will return there, you have only a few days left in the fort. 81

You have only a few days left in the fort, make sure you do not remove your shawl. Lovely woman, your family is highly honored. Do not think a single moment in the desert can be compared to your life here. Lady, preserve your honor, and you will go to Malir, oh Marui. 82

Your girlfriends, whose honor is unblemished, remember you. Do not get fat without your Maru, think of gold as lead. 83

Your girlfriends, whose honor is unblemished, remember you. There can be no questioning of their behavior." 84

The traveler who came from my ancestral land taunted me thus: "Do not sit on the beds wearing a fine necklace. Do not destroy the shawl of chastity, says Latif, that you wear around you. Your girlfriends have earnestly begged me to tell you to remain true. You will soon be summoned back with honor." 85

"How can the Marus be angry with me? My hair is sticky, and lice suck my blood. Sleep is poison to 86 my eyes as I remember the bushes of the desert. If they were here, they would realize how I have guarded my honor."

87 "Oh chaste one, much is still required of your chastity. Cut, slice, and mince yourself, and secretly let yourself be cooked. Preserve your virtue, so you may return to your country with honor."

88 "I will remain chaste, and I will not stay in the fort. The oyster is born in the ocean, it does not drink the river water. Just as it trusts in the cloud,[19] so is my heart fixed on Malir. The desert dwellers will drink milk if this captive returns.

89 Just as the oysters in the water live in reliance upon the cloud, and just as the cranes think of the mountains, so do I long for my home. I have made many promises to return; my heart hates it here. If I were not held prisoner in the fort, why would I stay?

90 The oyster is born in the ocean, its trust is in the cloud. The mollusk does not drink salt water, nor does it taste sweet water. It produces a pearl because it suffers in the deep.[20]

91 Oh my girlfriends, you should all learn the lesson of faithfulness from the oysters. Turning from other water, they wait trusting in the cloud.

The Maru has come from Malir and entered the fort. 92
My helper has returned, my oppressors have all become weak.

May you be at ease, traveler, with the dust where 93
you came from on your feet. Have you brought a message of love for Marui? Oh, how I long for that spinning place[21] and for that land. I reckon the dust of my native land to be the equal of musk.

How fine were the days I spent in confinement. In the 94
palace, I shed great tears like drops of rain. As I waited to be with him, I was torn into little pieces. My love has burnished my chains and made them gleam.

Oh Umar, today I met foragers from my homeland, 95
who stood and delivered messages from my beloved. By God's grace, says Latif, my iron fetters were removed.

When the ruler we rely on becomes a robber, how can 96
the Marus live in the desert, either now or in the future?

When he who is our support becomes a robber, at 97
whose door can the poor Marus complain?

May I die after bathing with the Maru in the Malir 98
river. I will return after washing myself in the

waters of my home. This will be a favor to the wearers of shawls in the desert.

99 I will have no other husband, the only one I favor is the one who wears a rough shawl. Although he may be dirty, my Maru is in my heart.

100 Let my face stay dirty, oh Sumiro, in case my Maru says: 'You washed it in the palace.'

101 Where there are woolen rugs, rough shawls, bags, huts, red berries, and fruits, my girlfriends are happy beside their husbands. If only I could enjoy the season's wild fruits with the Marus, this daughter of the desert would greet everyone among the thorn bushes."

102 If Marui were here I would ask about her.[22] I would approach Umar and make entreaties on her behalf. If he would not release her but kept her in confinement, I would offer myself. I would remove her chains, says Latif, and leave this place. I would set her free and take her by the arm to Malir. I would be her guide and take her to that lovely land.

103 "The knots in my heart that bind me to the Marus are like the ties of knotweed. Umar imprisons me with easy knots, says Latif. I will go to Malir and untie them, oh Sumiro.

My fetters are removed by hearing talk of my homeland. Sorrow and grief are removed from my heart and I am filled with joy. 104

From the very beginning, Umar, chastity was prescribed in your destiny. So you did not violate the honor of Marui, who was reared by the Marus. 105

Do not cry or scream, and do not shed tears. You are released from captivity, so burn your chains. Nomad girl, you will quickly reach the people of your tribe. 106

The wounds inflicted by the nomads are freshly opened today. Sorrows have come and found a place in my heart, oh Sumiro. My separation from the Maru has broken my bones." 107

Umar, I ask someone who is going, a traveler to the place where the Marus dwell. 108V
In the palace Marui weeps and makes others cry.
Turned aside from the way, the travelers get up and listen to what she says.
My soul wept when it remembered my kinsfolk.
No messenger from the nomads came yesterday.
Oh Sumiro, your kingdom has been entrusted to the lord.

16 *Kamod*

1 "You are a Samo prince, I am a Gandiri fishergirl who is full of faults. May you not change toward this Mangar girl on seeing the faces of the queens.

2 You are a Samo prince, I am a fishergirl, in whom there are countless faults. May you not change toward this Mangar girl on seeing a bit of fish oil.

3 You are Tamachi, lord of the landing place; I am a fishergirl of the Me caste. Do not reject me now that I have been given the title of your wife.

4 You are Tamachi, lord of the landing place; I am a poor fishergirl. I am close to you, my prince, so let my kinsfolk be exempted from tax."

5 Their baskets are full of stinking fish, and their trays are full of fish smell. It makes one ashamed if the edge of one's garment touches theirs. The Samo prince stands there and is kind to them.

6 They are dark, ugly, base, and in no way attractive. They sit beside the road with their baskets of stinking fish. Who besides the Samo can tolerate their coquetry?

7 They have lotus roots in their laps and wear garments made of lotus leaves. The king has come happily to their hut.

The fisherfolk are on close terms with Prince 8
Tamachi. The fisherwomen, young and old, come thronging to the palace. Whether they are from Lake Kinjhar or from far away, they have all been favored by him.

She does not cut fish, or sell them, or kill them, nor 9
does she set them beside her. She has deliberately thrown her basket into the well. She does things as they are done in the Samo's house.

She does not cut fish, or sell them, nor does she put 10
them in her basket. She does not place the scales in front of her to weigh them carefully. She does things as they are done in the Samo's house.

Nuri brought clothes made of lotus leaves and laid 11
them as an offering before him. The Samo ladies were all present in attendance upon him. He favored the fishergirl and took her with him in his carriage.

The fishergirl has no pride or arrogance in her heart. 12
She delighted the king with her eyes filled with graceful looks. Her artful ways won the Samo for her over all the others.

Nuri's helplessness was wonderfully hard to grasp. 13
The fishergirl charmed the Samo, who was the ruler of them all. Having lost their claims to him, the queens came and stood behind her.

14 In hands and feet, or in face and appearance, she is no fisherwoman. She is a queen among queens, like the main string on a lute. From the beginning she behaved like royalty. The Samo recognized this and tied the wedding band on her arm.

15 No one else on the Kinjhar lake has Nuri's beauty. She has been excused from the fishing gear, the landing places, and the boats. Tamachi stands there and waves the royal peacock fan over her.

16 Away with the royal women of the Samos and Sumiros, who come with heads held high. Bravo for the women born by the Kinjhar lake, who think of Tamachi. Instead of the queens, it is the Me girl who holds the jewel at night.

17 "May you live long, beloved; do not die, my smiling one. You are the comfort of my eyes, do not go from me. Tamachi, spend some time on the banks of Lake Kinjhar."

18 There is water below, fresh sprouting branches above, and trees all around. In the midst of all this, she comes and goes, to enjoy Tamachi. The north wind blows and makes Lake Kinjhar rock gently like a swing.

19 "There is water below, fresh sprouting branches above, and my beloved is beside me. So many of

my desires are fulfilled, none of them has been frustrated.

There is water below, fresh sprouting branches above, 20
and by the bank the lotuses swim. The spring breezes blow, and Lake Kinjhar is filled with fragrance."

The Samo queens adorn themselves and come to 21
delight the king. The prince carries a net and moves among the fishermen.

Tamachi was commanded to favor Nuri. He took the 22
fishergirl into his carriage and raised her status.[1] The Kinjhar people say this whole story is true.

Before she met the prince, Nuri and his high-born 23
ladies knew nothing of each other. They did not go together to marriage pavilions or to funerals, nor did they participate in weddings.[2] Relying upon Tamachi, what should they have to do with Lake Kinjhar?

The prince is not born of anyone, nor does he have any 24
issue. The fisherwomen, young and old, are all his kindred. *He does not give birth, nor is he born*[3] is the mark of his nobility and justice. Pride and glory distinguish the throne of Prince Tamachi.

Smarten up your huts, Prince Tamachi has come. 25
Banish your sorrows, fisherwomen, make your

courtyards shine. The Kinjhar people are full of calm; the Samo grants them his protection.

26 There is a magic in the Me girl's eyes that has speared the body of Prince Tamachi. What love has done is to make the prince carry a fishing net on his shoulders.

27V She sits among the fishmongers with diamonds in her hands.
As long as Tamachi lives, he shows his favor to Nuri.
He put foulness away and poured out floods of fragrance.
The blind and the lame came, when the generous one invited them.
See the generosity of the hero, who left no place unturned.
He gave treasures to the humble folk, like a first fruits offering.
He took out pearls and scattered them like cowries at the fish stall.
At the quayside he scattered gems like fish scales.
He gave gold away as alms and made a sport of silver.
He brought lustrous pearls with him and squandered rubies.
He made offerings of turquoises to the fakirs.
There, says Abdul Latif, he freely gave away priceless gems.

17 *Ghatu*

Those who knew much were confused, and the wits of 1
the heroes were blunted. Those who entered the
waters were drowned in the Indus. Former times
and times yet to come were forgotten in their
thoughts.

Their turbans are drenched in dew, and night has 2
fallen over them. Their oars have started to
wander, and their poles drift in the current. No
one has ever returned from Kalachi.

The whirlpool of Kalachi has a force that sweeps away 3
anyone who enters it. No one realizes why their
nets got tangled up.

Yesterday the turbaned fishermen went to Kalachi 4
with their fishing spears. The brothers have not
returned, and the kinsmen have been delayed.
That special company has been seized by the
churning whirlpool.

"I do not see their rafts in the water, nor are their nets 5
in place. Mother, the sailors have not brought
their boat home.[1]

I have seen so many of them killing lots of fish every 6
day. The fishermen's equipment in the house

saddens me. They have departed from the world and are lost in the deep water.

7 I stand in the warmth of the sun, gripped by the edge of the whirlpool. The fishermen have not come home, they have taken a very long time. Those in whom I trusted have turned away and sailed off in their boats.

8 There are heaps of sand where the fishermen looked for fish. Thousands of fishmongers have been ruined. The lake has dried up, and the tax collectors have left.[2]

9 I have had to borrow fish.[3] God bring back the fishermen. Almighty lord, do not let me be ashamed before the traders. My body has learned the worth of the fishermen, now that they are gone."

10 You stroll along in just the same way as the fishermen did. In their love for the whirlpool of Kalachi, they never slept for a moment.

11 In their search they fell into the whirlpool as they explored the deep water. With happy faces, the sailors slew the crocodile.

12 Crocodiles are not killed by casting nets upon still waters. Use large strong sea nets made with

colored twine. These are shallow waters and
channels, the deep swell is still some way out.

Perhaps the great fish has caught them. The fishermen 13V
have not come home.
Go, sailors, and attack. Vent your fury on the evil
creature.
Where are their hooks? Where are their nets?
The eddies make a fearful roar. Before you there is
foam.
Sisters, Abdul Latif says, they will all cross over the
deep water.

18 Ramakali

1 In this world there are yogis of light and yogis of
fire.[1] Their company is alight with love; I will not
survive without them.[2]

2 In this world yogis dwell in the warmth of love. They
have parted company with ease and keep distant
from comfort. They have created havoc in me; I
will not survive without them.

3 Oh, do not forget the yogis for a moment. Search
desperately for the footprints of the ascetics.
Look for the path they have followed and go after
them. Pursue them by night and day; I will not
survive without them.

4 The sound of the yogis' instruments is precious to me.
Their horns[3] are all made of gold, but regard their
detachment and do not speak of their wealth.[4]
Having gained your trust, they will suddenly leave
for the east.[5] Come, they have signaled to us; I will
not survive without them.

5 The instruments of the yogis are precious to me. They
are beyond conversation, they do not engage in
discussion. They have attained ecstasy; I will not
survive without them.

Or else bind me with ropes and take me with you. I 6
have understood the secrets of their community from the sound of their *surando*.[6] Now they are in my heart; I will not survive without them.

Their horns instantly removed the veil from my heart. 7
I am slain by their *surando*. They have killed me; I will not survive without them.

The yogis gather up their ego and set fire to it. The 8
masters use their horns to consume the self. They find a way to heal the sick; I will not survive without them.

When I see the lodge where they stayed I am 9
overcome by grief. The *surandos* of the ascetics are no longer heard at dawn. They live in accordance with divine will; I will not survive without them.

I lament in the place where they stayed, I cannot 10
control my voice. I am knifed by the *surando* of those followers of the divine.[7] Alas for their departure; I will not survive without them.

When I sit and look at them, I see nothing else. 11
Nobody possesses a beauty like theirs. When I look at it, I see nothing else; I will not survive without them.

12 Today the ascetics are not in their place. Consuming their ego, they have gone, and their feet did not touch the ground. "Alas, alas!" I cry in their lodge; I will not survive without them.

13 The ascetics have got rid of their ego. The naked ones possess the entire treasury of love. They are as fragrant as sandalwood; I will not survive without them.

14 The naked ones have gone to Hinglaj[8] to behold the goddess. The devotees of Shiv rejoice at the sight of Dwarka.[9] Their guide is Ali;[10] I will not survive without them.

15 Sitting by themselves, they take private counsel. The masters set out on their journey, deserting the place where they stayed. Their departure made me weep; I will not survive without them.

16 The yogis have destroyed their separate existence, their business is with the universal. The lodge where they stay is nonexistence; I will not survive without them.

17 On the first day[11] I realized something about the ascetics. They are not well for a moment, but suffer all the time. The sannyasis, says Shah, are in pain. Only through necessity do the yogis wander hidden in the world.

On the second day I sat and heard about the ascetics. 18
Their clothes are coated with dust, and the strings for tying up their hair are worn out. They have carefully arranged their matted braids and tied their topknots well. The poor creatures do not talk about their state to anyone. The naked ones are happy, they wander hidden in the world.

On the third day they kindle fire in the lodges where 19
they stay. The yogis gather sweepings and straw and set fire to them. The ascetics know all about burning. They do not speak of their secret, they wander hidden in the world.

On the fourth day they are sunk in thought as they 20
lean on their crutches. Slain by the idea of the beloved, what have they to do with falseness? Some commotion rages within the yogis. The masters have been turned into gold, they wander hidden in the world.

On the fifth day some anxiety torments them. The 21
yogis' hearts are gripped by pain. Assuredly they have alighted on the field of love. For them, says Shah, the whole night passes in suffering. Having beheld the beloved, they wander hidden in the world.

On the sixth day they are completely absorbed in 22
meditation. From the beginning God alone has

been in the yogis' hearts. They take ashes from the fire and rub them on their bodies. Begging for a little grain, they wander hidden in the world.

23 On the seventh day, says Shah, they wash their clothes. With folded arms they stand before God the unseen. They have brought signs of some great realm. Their souls are entwined in secret with Ram.[12] They take their rags, and they wander hidden in the world.

24 On the eighth day the yogis arise and go from place to place. The masters learned the ways suitable for yoga. Ram always dwells in their hearts. For some purpose they wander hidden in the world.

25 On the ninth day, their eyes are wakeful and bright. The merciful lord noticed them and showed his mercy. Their abode is wherever the lord appears. This is their sign, that they wander hidden in the world.

26 On the tenth day, see how they are adorned by the favor of the beloved. They have turned the pages of union, and they have grasped them. They have found the path of the guru, says Latif. The yogis have gained glory, they wander hidden in the world.

On the eleventh day the renouncers find fortune. Their pilgrimages are completed and they have entered the sacred enclosure. They have permanently kept silent, they wander hidden in the world. 27

On the twelfth day their hearts' desires are fulfilled. The yogis all long for this pilgrimage. They who find union with the guru are exalted. 28

They are always on a journey, roaming on the roads. They travel to the east, intoxicated as they go from land to land. They are aware of God the unseen; let us go and see where they stay. 29

Take nonbeing on your shoulders and do not be like those who are tied to existence. True yogis are not like this, says Latif. How can those who maintain the least connection with the world be called true ascetics? 30

The Kapat yogis[13] have their ears pierced and slit for earrings. As lovers, they sit forever facing the north wind. They fast and mortify their bodies. They are fakirs who have obliterated themselves; let us go and see where they stay. 31

The masters are roasted for the sake of the beloved, they are cooked and become kebabs. They regard 32 sin and merit as the same. Their eyes shed tears mingled with blood. How can you ask them about their caste?

33 The masters carry their horns on their shoulders; keeping any kind of company brings them nothing but grief. Some painful thought drives them toward Kabul.[14] The yogis were talking yesterday about a lodge there.

34 Master, your shelter stands before me like a thorn.[15] Oh naked one, why did you build it if you were going to leave it?

35 If you think of becoming a yogi,[16] then break all ties. Oh naked one, do not go to the house of your friends and wail. Go and beg from the band of yogis who understand but say that they do not.

36 If you think of becoming a yogi, then break all ties. Attach your heart to those who are not born and do not beget. Then you will get to the end of the field of love.

37 If you think of becoming a yogi, then control your mind and destroy it within. With your heart smoking with love, turn the beads of the rosary in your mind. Respectfully suffer all that the master wills.

If you think of becoming a yogi, then drink the cup of 38
nonbeing. Search out and grasp nonbeing, do not
stand there with ego. Then, oh seeker, you will
enjoy the full profit of oneness.

If you think of becoming a yogi, then seal your mouth 39
with rings. The ears you split countless times have
made no difference to you. Abandon your sheet
and put on bits of leather, shoes are not suitable
for you. Then, master, you will not be faulted
before the guru.

Yoga is proper for yogis, and it is yogis whom yoga 40
suits. Hidden secrets are contained in the soul of
yogis. Ah, alas for me that I did not learn yoga.

You are not worthy of yoga, why do you talk about it? 41
There is only one path to the beloved; you journey
over different country. The masters went toward
the beloved, shedding tears of blood.

The yogis are not alive, so do not live if you adopt 42
yoga. You fool, let your ears hear this message:
"Destroy your existence, keep away from the
self." This life is absolutely nothing, you clueless
creature, yet you still say "I."

Either become a yogi, you shameless creature, or else 43
quit their company. Why get your ears split if you

cannot endure the cold? Get out and be off with you, in case you disgrace the others.

44 Yogis are not friends or close to anyone. I have encountered those who talk of the east.[17] Day and night their gaze is fixed on the goddess.[18] They have aroused infinite longing in my heart, says Latif. Oh God who veils faults, may I be dyed with the divine in the company of the masters.

45 Yogis who search for food are false. Accursed are the wretches who look after their bellies.

46 Yogi, you have got your ears split, do not become a woman. Oh master, have you not heard how the brave sacrificed their lives? Ask what you need to ask; those who do not speak do not win the game. Go to that land, oh yogi, with helplessness to guide you.

47 Completely fill your heart with the smoke of love. Bring your life and burn it in love's fire. Oh creature, what you should do is to become water from fire.

48 Those ears on the side of your head do not hear straight. Use your inner ears to hear the message.

49 The knees of the sannyasis are like Mount Sinai.[19] The renouncers do not take their ego with them

to the east. The yogis are draped in the cloak of mysteries. They are covered from top to toe in closeness to the divine.

Their knees are a *mihrab*,[20] and their bodies are 50
a mosque. Their hearts point the direction
to Mecca, their bodies circumambulate the
Kaaba. Proclaiming the divine reality, they have
renounced the body. The guide is contained in
their hearts, how can they be held accountable for
sin?

The beloved's face is their *mihrab*,[21] the entire world is 51
their mosque. They have given up the Qur'an, and
the tablet telling right from wrong. Intellect and
knowledge take flight there. Everything is God;
where can I go and perform my intention to pray?

The fire of love blazes within them, while on the 52
outside they are covered with ashes like stokers.
Choosing a retreat, they have abandoned lies,
vices, and falseness. They have nothing to do with
sin, but practice many virtues. The more they
burn, the purer and the happier they become.

For what purpose do the yogis follow this path? 53
Their hearts are not set on hell, nor do they
desire paradise. They have nothing to do with
unbelievers, and they do not have Islam in their

minds. They stand there saying: “Make the beloved your own.”

54 Lack of expectation is the sheet in which the ascetics are wrapped. Those seekers are always happy with their destiny.

55 Lack of expectation is their sustenance, the sheet in which the ascetics are wrapped. Sometimes they are on horseback, sometimes they go on foot. The masters swim in the sea like a float. If they enter the mouth of the crocodile they do not say a word.

56 Those by whom the beloved passed become dyed in the color of love. The yogis have constructed their refuge place on the eddying waters of nonexistence. The silent ones used their divine knowledge to churn the whirlpool.

57 The yogis endure cold blasts, painful times, and gales in their minds. They have no refuge besides God.

58 Lack of desire is their hut, nonexistence is their refuge. Contentment is their kingdom, they ask for nothing else.

59 The masters are slaughtered by a knife that removes their happiness. By day their bodies are in

pain, and they suffer all night long. Mother, the community of yogis is always sick.

Ram dwells in their soul, they speak of nothing else. 60
They filled the cup of love and drank deeply from it. After that they closed their lodges and left.

With matted braids over their foreheads, the yogis are 61
always lamenting. No one has ever spoken to ask what makes them grieve. They spend their entire life in suffering.

They have spent years sitting with their foreheads 62
dirty with dust. Their eyes are directed toward God the unseen, they never turn toward the earth. Scorched by fire, their hair has become gray instead of black. They tremble, says Latif, and they shed tears of blood. They do not leave their love, being happy to pass their time in pain.

It was not the naked ones who bowed to their lord, but 63
their love that made them bow before him. The rain of divine favor fell on the huts of the whole community of yogis.

They do not bow down to the lord, nor does the lord 64
make them bow down. They do not make yoga an object of pilgrimage or worship. The yogis bring

the precious gems of spiritual knowledge as their tokens.

65 They worship Shiv all the time, and wash their loincloths every day. Those who have not killed their lower self find no favor with the lord.

66 Wearing quilts, the yogis spend time together with bells tied to their sides. They keep their bodies free from impurity. The naked ones do not sleep, but go weeping toward Ram.

67 Their sticks and kindling are like jasmine flowers. I die longing for those masters whose quilts contain roses. The yogis are priceless within, but look ugly on the outside.

68 Standing to one side of the bazaar, the yogis in their quilts remember the guru. They recite divine verses and pay the price for the draught of love in full. Their faces look sweet as they are overcome by the intoxication of love.

69 The yogis are disgusted by eating, they are not greedy for food. Crying out in the wilderness, they do not spend even a moment begging. Seeking adversity, they arise and keep company with suffering.

70 They do not carry a bowl to beg with, nor do they ask for anything from people's houses. Worshipers

of Shiv, they stand far from people's homes. Why should they ask about the religious law when the court is within them?[22]

If those who carry a bowl and beg only realized, they would receive alms in the desert without begging for a single moment. 71

Those who are restless late at night sleep in the evening. The yogis, says Latif, start up at midnight. Seeing the world asleep, they set off on their travels. Which way should they stretch out to rest when God is present everywhere? 72

In the afternoon they stay sitting, in the evening they remain asleep. They starve and are dying of hunger, but they do not beg from anyone. They have not accustomed their stomachs to feel hunger and taste delicacies. All the fakirs beg for is the medicine that induces silence. 73

They have made their bodies thin by binding them with leather bands. They have not accustomed their stomachs to feel hungry and taste delicacies. This is the way that the yogis come to Kabul.[23] 74

Bidding farewell, the yogis have departed from this place. In their hearts they have imagined a distant land. Covered in new apparel, the renouncers have wandered on. 75

76 The yogis have reverence in their eyes. They have no ancestry or lineage, no mother or father. In all circumstances the beloved inhabits the soul of the masters. They keep no possessions other than their loincloth.

77 Those who wear the loincloth around them do not perform ablutions.[24] They have heard the call to prayer that preceded Islam.[25] Abandoning all other support, the masters are united with Gorakhnath.[26]

78 Do not let yourself be worshiped, oh yogi, curses on people's devotion. Oh renouncer, says Latif, keep your mouth from pretense. Kill your mind and destroy it; then you will see a refuge at the sacred bathing place.

79 Do not let yourself be worshiped, oh yogi, but maintain your yoga. Oh master, to make people your servants is a great fault. There is no life of luxury for those who flee the world, which true ascetics leave behind.

80 The patient ones were with you for the night; in the morning they will go. Preserve their memory in every fiber of your being, says Latif. It will be difficult to be with the yogi community a second time.

Talk with them while they are in their lodge. Devote 81
yourself to them ten times a day. With luck you will meet again with the yogis who have gone to Hinglaj.

Sit with them while they are in their lodge. The 82
masters have gone on a journey, their thoughts are on a distant land. Abandoning the comfort of their own country, they have eagerly gone to the Ganga.

In the lodge today[27] there is no gathering of the yogis. 83
Think of the sannyasis and weep as much as you wish. See, from your side those spiritual beings have departed.[28]

In the lodge today the seekers do not talk. The yogis 84
have got up and left; their lodges are the death of me. The restorers of my soul to life, those spiritual beings, have departed.

In the lodge today there is no assembly of the yogis. 85
When I remember them I am consumed and reduced to a heap. My mind was directed to them, those spiritual beings have departed.

In the lodge today those who wept aloud are not 86
there. The yogis who took no ease and who were the lodge's adornment are absent. They have closed their lodge, which now lies silent, and no

instruments play there. The naked ones have departed, and none of the easterners remains. When I think of the sannyasis I am overwhelmed by waves of grief. Those spiritual beings have bound their minds with ropes.

87 Today there is no smoke or flame[29] in the lodge. After giving me the taste for their company, the renouncers have departed. Mother, I have been killed by the tears that the yogis have made me shed.

88 Being with the yogis has brought us to life and removed our grief. They offered the blind the way to the east.

89 Alas, if they were here, I should perhaps have had a claim on them. If only I could find their rosary beads, their form, and their wisdom, all of which I have forgotten.

90 The yogis have filled their bags with hunger and rejoice. They have no desire for food, they pour out thirst and drink it. Those spiritual beings, says Latif, have made pulp of their minds. The masters have crossed the wilderness and drawn near to habitation.[30]

91 They have no covering or quilt, nor the least scrap of a loincloth. The lord is before them wherever they step.

The naked ones have tied the loincloth of love around them. As they came into the world, so they have returned. Their true status will be revealed in the east. 92

If people looked for the spiritual path in the way that they look for bread, they would have crawled and found the way, says Latif, and their pain would be removed. 93

For the yogis, hunger and thirst are like the celebrations of ordinary people. The intoxicated faqirs observe the fast, the ascetics stay away from Eid. 94

God is still far away from the sannyasi who is concerned about clothing and food. 95

You sit thinking of last year; do something now about going. Die today, oh yogi; everyone will die tomorrow. 96

Leaving the settlement on Mount Ganjo,[31] they eagerly set out. They have finished off their bodies on the path directed by the guru. Those yogis have not sat down and rested on the way. While traveling, they met Ram and were spared the rest of the journey. 97

98 The sannyasis' eyes always shine with tears like the moon. The yogis stop their eyes from sleeping and they remain awake.

99 There are still yogis who are worthy of their horns. They are sitting and playing, if you would hear them, oh sannyasi.

100 Those who have accepted dying[32] do not forget the one lord. Those naked ascetics do not sleep on the way. Their eyes are always bright and vigilant.

101 Searching is very difficult, do not search without a lamp. Remain in your cell for as long as your beloved lives. Leave the lodge only when he departs.

102 Do not search without a lamp, searching is very difficult. Hundreds and thousands and millions have been blinded by this darkness.[33]

103 What you thought was a lamp is the brilliance of the sun. For the blind it is still dark when night passes and turns into day.

104 The yogis did not look at the place where the abode of the lord is. The yogis with misguided faith traveled on a long journey. He is here, but they went in vain to Hinglaj.

The yogis did look[34] at the place where the abode of 105
the lord is. The yogis with rightly guided faith traveled on a long journey. He is right here, and they found him in Hinglaj.

Oh yogi, give no importance to what is only 106
transitory.[35] The field where Ali fought[36] is fine for sannyasi.

Those who are dyed in love of the lord have no 107
attachment to fine clothing. Those spiritual beings roam about in poor clothes, says Latif.

Hunger is the charity for which they beg, ashes are 108
the perfume they bathe in. They have chosen an appearance that ordinary people are ashamed of.

Horns, strings, and quilts—these three they have 109
abandoned, along with their sacred threads. They have thrown their begging bowl to the ground and smashed it to pieces. Those who have become attached to the divine spirit never emerge from their cells.

Curses on your quilts and coverings, set your blankets 110
on fire. Lower your eyes before those who truly practice yoga. Realize that that the horn you hold disgraces you.[37]

The quilt the guru gave me is my pride. Oh disciple, sit 111
cross-legged and wear it with reverence.

112 It would be disgraceful to remove the quilt given by the guru. How many of its blessings will the disciple be able to recite?

113 The quilt given by the guru adorns me greatly. If you wear it with reverence, it will take you on the path.

114 Quilts[38] inside and silk outside—yogis of this sort are slaves of donkeys.

115 Silk inside and quilts outside—yogis of this sort are slaves of God.

116 You who wear a quilt, do not look at all the flowers and think that they are many. Recognize him as the one in everything.

117 See, they have thrown their begging bowls on the ground and put aside their staffs. They have passed beyond impurities and have not turned back into base metal. They have quit the sensations of this world and have become one with the universal.

118V Their horn is a mystery.[39] Sometime it will kill me.
It is not like the pipe the camel men play.
It wipes out the flute, and the gourd[40] is not its equal.
It is not like the buffalo bells that brought Suhini across.[41]

It is sharper than the strings that severed Diyach's
head.[42]
There is nothing like it in the north, in Sindh, or in
Hind.[43]
Those who have tasted it say it is sweeter than sweets.
Go when you hear it, do not just sit there but step out.
Those who have heard it playing become masters
without ego.
How can one praise something that God has extolled?
It far surpasses thousands of other instruments.
Large bells charm wild beasts, but it enchants men.
Sisters, says Abdul Latif, it brings the dead to life.

19 Khahori

1 With silent prayer, the Khahoris have searched and found the divine. With these syllables[1] the lovers have passed the stage of infinity. United with the divine, they have become divine, baked by their master. To them everything appears divine.

2 Mother, I have seen those who have seen the beloved. One should come and stay for a night with those heroes. Knowing them with loving respect acts as a raft over the world's deep water.

3 Groups of Khahoris went to the Pab range. I ask you, traveler, where can I find those foragers? They have searched the mountains after spending the night in the wilderness.

4 Why did you make no effort at all early this morning? The Khahoris left at dawn with their water pouches. How will you get plants from distant lands?

5 The foragers search for the place that no one has heard of or been told about. The ascetics snatch their rest upon the stones. They search for true knowledge in the land where there are no limits.

The adepts wander with their bodies covered with 6
dust. They do not speak openly to the ignorant.
They possess secret knowledge about my beloved.

Go then into the courtyard of the Khahoris. Hidden 7
from the world, they have filled their hearts with
passion. Because of their pain, the foragers do not
sleep and enjoy rest.

The plants the foragers gather do not grow less. They 8
bring signs of that world near to us. Afterward
they speak of the beloved.

Anyone who forages for plants finds it hard to search 9
in the mountains. The rock gives no gifts to those
who are asleep.

I have seen the Khahoris who spend no time in houses. 10
Attached to God the one, they weep and shed
tears in the cold of the night. Ever since they have
been engaged in foraging, they have endured
sorrows.

Fastening their bundles, the Khahoris left with 11
them at dawn. Searching in the mountains, they
have reduced themselves to dust. Making their
bodies suffer, they have found their goal in the
mountains.

12 They do not take strong animals to ride as they go on their distant way. The foragers proceed to the bushes in search of some special plant. The mark of the Khahoris is that the clothes they wear are all torn.

13 Their faces are dried up, they wear old shoes on their feet. In their search they have reached a place where even guides are lost. These mysterious ones speak of the mysteries of that distant land.

14 They carry dried-up water pouches under their arms and wear rope sandals on their feet. Have you met any Khahoris with eyes streaming with tears?

15 Those who got to know about the settlement on Mount Ganjo left their flourishing crops in their search for God.[2]

16 Those who became aware of the settlement on Mount Ganjo closed up all their books in their desire for God.

17 Those who caught the scent of the settlement on Mount Ganjo gave up all their clothing and became desirous of God.

18 What business have you with the settlement on Mount Ganjo? When you see that rock, you get no peace. Do not search in the mountains. Why

wander in the world? To become a Khahori, give up everything and burn it.

This place where there are no tracks of birds is out of this world. There the Khahoris wander, picking their food from the trees. 19

Where there are no tracks of birds, there a bonfire[3] burns. Who else would light it besides a company of Khahoris? 20

Those who have abandoned the way of the world have come into trouble. They who possess true vision are blind as they cross the deserts. Blocking their ears, they wander as if dumb. The pain of the sentence of separation affects the deaf. They became renouncers for the sake of the divine, which they yearn for even when asleep. The Khahoris' desire never leaves them. 21

Those who lost their way look and search in the mountains. Learning from the lost path, they do not proceed along the right track. Abandoning both worlds, they do not ask about the correct route. The poor creatures throw dust on themselves for the sake of the beloved. The Khahoris possess some knowledge of the divine. 22

Few travelers have set foot in this pathless wilderness. 23
Wherever men wander lost is where the path to

the beloved lies. Only one person in a million finds a trace of that country.

24 In being guided there are many snakes; being lost is like honey. Awareness comes to the one who wanders away from them both.

25 After traveling from land to land, mother, the Khahoris have come. How do I know where the dust on the feet of those heroes comes from?

26 Those who traveled in the jungle were not lost, those who traveled on the road were not robbed. Those who quit both worlds did not find themselves lost.

27 The jungle will cry out in tears to the hunters. It will get up and say: "There are no dogs or traps." Afterward there will never be a jungle like it in the world.

28 How excellent is that deserted jungle, in which only the beloved dwells. Abandon the place where there are millions of evil men.

29 The night is dark, the day is bright—these are the qualities of natural light. There is no color or form where the beloved is present.

30 Even today the dust they raised as they passed through the mountains can still be seen. The

foragers come for the wild grain that grows in the wilderness. Today the tents of the Khahoris are no longer here.

True Khahoris are known only to the birds that seek 31
them out and make their nests in their courtyards.

I am of low caste. Recognize yourself, beloved. 32V
I spend the whole night filling the pots of those ascetics.
If they graciously call me their slave girl, then I am fortunate.
I will continue wandering in the mountains until it is dawn.
I will make my supplication to God when day breaks.
Sisters, Abdul Latif says, I communicate with the beloved.

20 *Purab*

1 Performing humble obeisances, oh crow, fall at the beloved's feet. On the way do not forget the message I am giving you. For God's sake, says Latif, speak to him in secret. Repeat what I tell you, crow, and be happy.

2 Fly to me, crow, and tell me his messages. Sit down here and say a little about our time together. Fly and bring me the beloved, even though he is physically far away.

3 Sit on the branch and tell me his message, says Latif. Do not turn away from the excellent practice of your race.[1] Fly and bring me the beloved, who is so brilliant in appearance.

4 Come back quickly, crow, and proclaim "He has returned." Even if he has gone to Kalat,[2] fly and bring me the beloved.

5 Call the beloved, crow, even if he has gone to distant lands. Without having him in the world, my eyes have no more tears to shed. For God's sake, says Latif, come to my village and celebrate. Even if the beloved has been hurt in some way and is angry, fly and bring him to me.

If the beloved is in a foreign land, give me news of him, oh crow. I will completely cover your wings with gold. Circle over his house, and give the beloved my messages. 6

Oh crow, with my hands I will take out my heart and give it to you. Go to the beloved's country and consume it in his presence, so that he may ask who offered him this sacrifice. 7

Oh crow from my beloved, come and give me a message of delight. You smell of spring and of pounds of musk and perfume. Circle high above the beloved's courtyard. When I see you, I am happy and am cleansed of suffering. 8

Today the crow has brought me streams of happy messages from the beloved. My desires have been accomplished, and my being is filled with joy. God has brought my loved one to me, and my cries have been answered. 9

Crow, your movements have revived my sick body. After treading on other branches, you sing upon a double bough. Fly up from the branch, so that my beloved may come home. 10

Crow, take my message to the beloved. "My darling, some strong reason has delayed you. Without you 11

I am hard pressed, and sit overcome by the pain of separation."

12 With the beloved absent abroad, the pain of separation has strengthened its grip on me. My eyes are turned toward the beloved and are watching the path that leads to the village, for travelers to bring me happy news.

13 Crow, I am indebted to your race. Fly at dawn toward the beloved, says Abdul Latif. Utter many entreaties and implore him greatly, saying: "Beloved, we cannot find anyone like you in the world."

14 The beloved's crow struts upon the bough. He has brought good news and smiles. He is the one who delivered my message to him. He is welcome to walk upon my eyes, for he is a member of my beloved's court.

15 The eyes that the beloved raises when he laughs give me joy. He banishes all sorrows when he smiles. People think it is hunger that makes ascetics thin, but it is actually the pains of love.

16 You call yourself a yogi but desire comfort; you have learned nothing. You sit down in exhaustion while still at the start of your journey. You have not come close to your guru but proclaim that you

have been rewarded with his favor. You should unceasingly remain dedicated to the beloved.

The yogis from the east shut down their camp and left in the middle of the night. At dawn I did not hear the cries of the sannyasis. Such is the nature of yogis, who have no ties to those who suffer. 17

They set out on their way and proceeded toward the east. They will give up these homes and settle in others that lie ahead. 18

"Oh, the east, the east!" I cry, when my heart is filled with thoughts of them. As I long for the beloved, my eyes flood with tears. I am wounded by the pain of thinking that I will not hear of the beloved or meet him. 19

Lord, may my connection with the yogis not be broken. 20V
The yogis told me to travel to Hinglaj.
The ascetics took me to the land of the east.
That is the goal of my pilgrimage, and my resting place; that is my journey.
The masters have shown me my place of pilgrimage and my resting place.

21 *Karayal*

1 As it flew up, it uttered the cry *He is one*.[1] It passed through the fog where birds are tested.

2 Parting company with the cranes, it flew up high in the sky. It flew toward the lake where its beloved dwells.

3 With its eyes upon the ocean, it stands looking at the deep water. The wild goose is familiar with the pearls that lie in the depths.

4 Will you not plunge into the depths for the pearls? Oh wild goose, what business do you have on the bank?

5 Now it has come into the presence of the lake and has become aware of what it contains. The bird has discovered treasure in its depths.

6 The clear water has been churned up by the cranes. When the wild geese arrive, they die of shame.

7 If you once take a careful look at the wild geese, you will never associate with the cranes again.

8 Fly here, oh wild goose, to the lake where they think of you, in case the hunters plan a trick to kill you.

The roots of the lotus go down to the bottom, the bee 9
flies around in the sky.[2] The divine provider has brought their affair to fruition. Praise be to that love which has brought the lovers together.

The roots of the lotus go down to the bottom, the bee 10
flies around in space. Their affair is a symbol of love. Their thirst is not quenched, however much they each drink.

While people sleep, the wild geese fly. They examine 11
the jewels in the deep and choose them. What can the hunters with their tricks do to them?

The peacocks are all dead; not one wild goose is left. 12
This lake has now become the home of false birds.

He is the bird, the cage, the lake, and the wild goose. 13
When I looked within myself, I realized that the hunter whom the body fears[3] prowls about inside me.

Do not think the cobra's brood to be weak little 14
snakes.[4] When they strike, even the elephant cannot move from where it is.

The snakes that dwell in the desert possess a deadly 15
poison. Their faces are like angels, but their bite never fails. If you brush by them, you do not have the slightest chance.

16 The snakes that dwell in the desert possess a special kind of poison. Even a thorn touched by their venom has a deadly effect. Snakes of that kind are well known in every country. Who would care to battle with them?

17 Even peacocks turn away from some kinds of cobra. If by cunning the snakes do manage to bite them, the peacocks all retreat. They withdraw all their companies, thinking the snakes deadly.

18 Only a fool provokes a cobra. No one who gets bitten by them comes back for more. Either they die on the spot or they pine for recovery.

19 Oh snake, you have made great enemies of the snake-charming yogis. Oh serpent, you will not escape, you have entered great danger. This is the abode of those who set fire to Junagarh.[5]

20V It is for just a little while, this flattery.
The game is false, and false is the display.
You climb upon the branch and twitter, foolish bird.
Have you not heard how the eagle pounces?

22 *Sarang*

The sky is overcast, says Latif, look at the clouds. 1
Heavy drops of rain are falling; drive your livestock outside. Leave the lowlands for higher ground, taking your things with you. Do not abandon your trust in God.

God has covered the sky, says Latif, look at the clouds. 2
The downpour has filled the plains with freshness. God who is one has increased the growth of the grass on the paths. Fresh spirit fills the herdsmen as the water rains down to remove their sorrows.

The overcast sky is not as beautiful as a sight of the 3
beloved. Without the beloved, says Shah, this spectacle gives no pleasure to the soul. Once my beloved comes to my pasture ground, it is as if thousands of rainy seasons were there.

Once my beloved comes to my pasture ground, my 4
heart is filled with peace. Sorrows quickly leave us. The beloved has let us see him plainly.

Today the rain bird[1] utters its cry toward the north. 5
The peasants prepare their plows, the herdsmen are happy. Today my beloved has taken on the form of the rain.

6 Today clouds hang in the north like long black hair. To signal the rain, flashes of lightning have come like brides dressed in scarlet clothes.[2] My beloved is far away, but the rain has brought me close to him.

7 Today I hope for clouds in the sky. Friends, when I see the rainy season I think of my beloved. I am hopeful that the rains may soak the earth. All I want is to have you in the house throughout this season.

8 The rains have swept down with a great noise from the north. The ponds and low-lying ground are filled with water, forming streams that flow. Behold the musklike perfume in the plains. These are the same rains that fall on the Prophet's holy tomb.[3]

9 Suddenly the beloved has let us see him. The rust has been wiped from my heart, which is filled with joy. All my heart's desires have been fulfilled since I saw my beloved.

10 Oh rain, if you learn to pour like my eyes, perhaps you will not stop shedding your drops throughout the days and nights.

11 There are rich stores in the village granaries, lightning flashes in the clouds. All pains are dispelled on seeing how the beloved behaves. May the rains pour cascades upon the lover in the evening.

There are Arab horses in the courtyard, outside there are buffaloes with twisted horns. On the open ground the huts look good. The bed is perfumed, my beloved is at my side, and how sweetly the rain falls. May the days always be like this for me and my beloved. 12

It has rained in the plains and deserts, it has rained on the lower ground. At dawn the sound of the churning sticks is heard on the plains. The prosperous farmers' wives rejoice, and their hands are full of butter. They milk the happy buffaloes that stand before them. Both maids and mistresses look happy in their huts. 13

It has rained in the plains and deserts, it has rained in Jaisalmer.[4] The sky is overcast and the rains have come to the desert. Women left on their own have lost their worries, says Latif. The paths have been made fragrant, and the herdsmen's wives are happy. 14

It has rained in the plains and the deserts, it has rained toward Kachchh.[5] See how the level ground is covered with streams at dusk. God who forgives faults has removed troubles from the land. 15

Oh rain, for God's sake have a thought for those who thirst. Make the waters on the level ground abundant, and make the price of grain cheap. Fill 16 the land with rain, so that the herdsmen may be happy.

17 The rain is remembered by men, by deer, and by buffaloes. The ducks are sustained by the clouds and rain birds sing their songs. The shells in the sea wait for it every day. Give the herdsmen rainwater to drink so that they may be happy.

18 The rains are marked by lines[6] like the redness of lac. The clouds are marked by patterns like those printed on a shawl. It has rained over Bhit and filled the pools of Kirar.[7]

19 The rains have filled the sky and have come rejoicing to Bhit. The north wind brings flowerlike flashes of lightning. The greenery is fragrant, and grass is piled in heaps. Spread all over the level ground, the water has filled the pools of Kirar.

20 It has filled the pools of Kirar and rained upon the Variyasu[8] desert. It has come with the lightning to create a lovely season. Coming from Makani, it has rained upon Mount Pab. The creator has caused fresh grass to grow in abundance on the edge of the rivers and the hills.

21 The rains have made the fresh grass grow on the edge of the hills and have made the flowers grow beside the Garang channel. Proceeding from Hadakut,

the rain has filled the lowlands. The water overflows and everything grows flourishingly.

Today the peaks of the clouds have put forth wonderful colors. At night the desert is filled with the sound of fiddles, lutes, and other instruments. The rainy season has poured buckets of water over Padham lake. 22

The rains are synonymous with love.[9] If the rainy season puts on the appearance of raining, the clouds cry out. I will become like the cloud if you show you are intending to come. 23

They cry out thinking of their husbands, and they weep when they see the clouds. May the huts the widows built without their husbands not get soaked. If the north wind blows them down, to whom can they cry out? May their husbands return to protect them. 24

They cry out thinking of their husbands, and they sob when they see the clouds. Their hearts tremble when they hear the roar of the thunder. Helpless without their husbands, they are struck dumb. 25

Elephants learn their graceful gait[10] from the movement of the clouds. The scarlet ladybugs are astonished when they see the redness of his lips.[11] The flashes of lightning laugh, glittering like the 26 full moon. Everyone is longing to see the beloved, says Latif. He has gathered saffron[12] and taken it away with him.

27 The season of the rains has come, and the musical gathering is assembled. The rains are pouring down. Grass is growing in lowlands, where many buffaloes graze. The herdsmen's wives happily weave themselves garlands. The plants and vegetation grow abundantly. May you remove days of sorrow from the world.

28 May God bring you to me, my dear beloved. My life is given to thinking of you; in longing it heaves sighs.

29 Like the rains of Savan,[13] my beloved comes in the form of clouds. He dwells near those who have spent their whole life longing for him.

30 I need protection and covering, but my hut cannot keep out the cold. Tell my fine husband what a state I am in. Come to my courtyard, beloved, so that I may feel better.

31 I seek your protection, husband, for I die of cold in the evening. Oh perfect one, I shiver from the cold in my cotton covering. I endure in the hope that my husband will return at dawn.

I seek your protection, husband, for I die of cold all 32
night. Oh perfect one, I do not sleep a wink in my
cotton covering. If you are back by dawn I will not
think of the cold.

With the coming of the rains, the beloved thunders 33
near Jhok.[14] The abundant rain he brings covers
the plains with colorful grass. Raining from his
eyes, he gives people pure water to drink.

The west wind brings flashes of lightning from the 34
direction of Khambhat.[15] He drives the buffaloes
with twisted horns on their path and sets the
calves upon their way. The herdsmen are happy,
their thirst and the heat are removed. The sudden
rain will soak the plains.

The sun does not shine bright and clear through the 35
clouds. The lightning reveals itself and brings
glad tidings to the people. Do not be downcast, oh
heart, the beloved will soon be with you.

The lightning descended on the Dhat desert and made 36
the plains green. The sun and moon are not to be
compared with his face. The beloved who dwells
in my heart has entered my home.

The lightning descended on the Dhat desert and was 37
bountiful. God showed the buffaloes abundant

favor. Oh my beloved, guard the honor of the herdsmen.

38 The cloudy skies have returned and have once again made it rain. All around and in every direction[16] storms of lightning have come to announce the rain. Some have arisen and gone to Istanbul, some have proceeded to the west. Some flash over China, some take care of Samarkand. Some have wandered to Rum, some to Kabul, some to Kandahar. Some go to Delhi, some to the Deccan, some thunder over Girnar. Some have busied themselves over Jaisalmer, some have rained over Bikaner. Some have drenched Bhuj, some have descended on the Dhat desert. Some have passed over Umarkot and have made the ground green. Oh my God, make Sindh flourish forever. Dear friend and sweet beloved, make the whole world prosperous.

39 Once again the rainy season has been prepared. Lightning storms have come to rain and cause most wonderful floods. There is an abundance of grain in the world. The rains have removed want, and the land is filled with prosperity.

40 The cloud was commanded to prepare the season of the rains. Lightning storms have come to make the rain pour down. Those who hoarded to make food dear are now wringing their hands.

As they turned the pages of their books, five would become fifteen.[17] May all hoarders and all oppressors perish. The farmers have again spoken of plentiful rain. Everyone is supported by your favor, says Shah.

The clouds gather in the heart, even though there is no cloud outside. The lightning brings rain to those who are filled with love. The eyes of those who have the beloved in their homes are never dry. 41

The clouds have flown from the north and come to rain. The rains have brought my once distant beloved close to me. 42

The season of the rains has come, and I will put on scarlet clothes. 43V
Today my beloved has appeared as the rains.
As the young woman hangs on the buffalo calves, her lovely hair is soaked.
Come to my hut, beloved, and take notice of me, says Shah.

23 Rip

1 Mother, my heart is drowned in suffering. Those who are in pain find honor in traveling along the path.

2 I am plunged into suffering. My beloved has taken away my well-being. Mother, I have been slain by separation from the one I love.

3 Suffering has no hands or feet, the pain of love operates internally. Pains line up to make their way inside the body. Who like me can endure a lonely life without the beloved?

4 Vegetation sprouts afresh in low-lying ground after it has rained. In the same way, suffering proliferates when the beloved is absent.

5 Open your heart to those who know its secrets, do not reveal them by weeping. Endure your sorrows until you find someone who can remove them.

6 Weep in secret, do not reveal your pain while you are apart from the beloved. Be strong in your sufferings like the edges of the lotus leaves.[1]

7 Like a herd of camels, my heart does not stay still for a single day. Nothing can break the love between me and my beloved.

I restrain my heart at every moment, but it cannot exist for a moment without him. The more I stop it sorrowing, the more it is plunged into grief. 8

I have clouds inside my head, and my eyes do not clear. Today the beloved has caused a deluge within my heart. Come, my love, and take notice of me. I am overwhelmed by the pain of being apart. 9

What shall I do with clouds? It is inside me that it rains. The overcast sky created by my beloved does not clear all day long. 10

When my beloved comes to mind, I disclose my secret love to him. All over my body my veins sound like the strings of a rebab. 11

My mind does not stay happy, nor is it restrained by reproaches. My heart is always covered with dust like a tree beside the road. 12

I rouse my heart when I emerge at dawn. Love always calls it back to the beloved's path. 13

When I recall him, he comes to mind. When I forget him, he is forgotten. He makes me hurt all the time, like a broken bone. 14

15 I will think of everything the beloved has done, to tell him about it. When he comes before me, I will forget it all.

16 If I do not get to be with my beloved, who else should I tell my secret to? My thoughts keep growing like the grass upon a riverbank.

17 My thoughts have grown into a tree inside me. I did not tell them to anyone else, and I could not be alone with my beloved.

18 My beloved is many-colored, like a blouse made of silk. He drives my mind mad; how can I forget him?

19 Like the eddies in the water created by the blade of an oar, my whole being is filled with thoughts of how I can meet him.

20 Like the water from a Persian wheel that comes out mixed with sand, I cannot separate my heart from my beloved however hard I try.

21 The cold is fierce, and I have no quilt or shelter. I have no partner and no sustenance; my youth has wasted away. What is the state of those whose huts have no support?[2]

The north wind blows hard, and I have no quilt or 22
covering. How will those whose huts have no
support cope with the cold?

The north wind blows in blasts, and I have no quilt or 23
covering. I have spent the whole night trying to
tuck the four edges of my shawl around me.

Why do you not cover your love like a kiln filled with 24
pots? If the flame escapes, how will the pots be
fired? Pay close attention to what the potters do.

Why do you not cover your love like a kiln filled with 25
pots? If the flame escapes, how will the pots be
fired? Act in the same way as the potters.

Learn love from the kiln. It burns all day long but 26
gives out no steam.

When people are asleep, I close my eyes like the kiln. I 27
am extinguished, but then I burn when I think of
you, beloved.

The wretches would die if they knew the least bit 28
about what the potters kneaded with the clay.
There would be mourning in this courtyard.

Do not remove the support of the one who shows 29V
favor to the ignorant.

Beggar, sit at the door of the giver and lay down your
burden.
He is nearer than near, so why utter these appeals?
He sits beside the dirty, he cleans out the foul.
What do faults in the imperfect matter before his
generosity, you fool?
What is the point of making a raft when he is there?
From the time of Adam he has created everyone out
of clay.
In our difficulties, Ali says, the beloved answers our
call.

24 *Barvo Sindhi*

Why did you go and become the slave of others? Take hold of the merciful lord of the world. He whose love is for God will be happy. 1

Just as the reed lets out melodious cries when it is being cut,[1] so do I lament the sudden pain I feel for my beloved. Doctor, why do you brand my arm, when it is my heart that feels the pain? 2

Like an elephant humbly touching the ground with its trunk, I use my head to move toward my beloved. In this way, says Latif, my body is joined to him, and I achieve closeness to him. 3

A lover's state cannot be described in words, says Latif. Fate so arranged things that my eyes shed floods of tears. Yesterday the beloved departed, but still be patient, oh heart. 4

Some beloveds are near but far, some are far but near. Some are never remembered, some are completely unforgotten. The beloved curls around my heart like the twists in a buffalo's horn. 5

Today the beloved called me and slaughtered me with his eyes. He shared out my flesh and left the skeleton. Saying, *Take counsel with the truth and take counsel with patience,*[2] he killed me, who was 6 already dead. The beloved laughed and left me wounded.

7 Men ask for wealth; I ask for the beloved all the time. For him I would immediately sacrifice the whole world. Just his name makes me happy, seeing him is still a long way off.

8 Sometimes the beloved closes his doors, sometimes they are left open. Sometimes I come and do not manage to enter, sometimes he invites me in. Sometimes I long for his call, sometimes he shares his secrets with me. This is what my beloved lord is like.

9 Though very handsome in appearance, their behavior is like the bitter apple.[3] Anyone who is attracted to them is consumed and dies.

10 Beloved, you are glorious and understanding. Be gracious to me in equal measure, my dearest. You are perfect, so how great a task is it for you to favor me with your glance?

11 Beloved, desire for you fills my heart. Take the knife and cut my limbs, do not stand on ceremony. I will think it a favor on your part if you look at me straight.

Beloved, it is not right for you to kill me, then not 12
return to ask how I am. All the blood in my body
has frozen because of my ecstatic love for you.
It is to you that we have secretly offered acts of
worship.

When I remember being with the beloved, I suddenly 13
utter cry upon cry.

Just as the blacksmith fixes links within links to form 14
a chain, so does my heart firmly fix its connection
with the beloved.

When the beloved emerges in his grace and walks 15
along, the very earth says *bismillāh*[4] and kisses the
path on which he goes. The houris stand in great
respect in a place of wonder. I swear by God that
the beloved is more beautiful than everything.

Oh, the world is passing, passing, and never the same 16
for a moment. My dear, they will kick up the dust
with their feet to make your grave. The spade and
the measuring stick[5] are waiting for everyone.

Today my limbs were stamped by my beloved's hand.[6] 17
The pains of separation treat me like the stone
flail that beats the corn.

18 Today my fortune favored me: the beloved came and entered my door. Joys came and gave griefs a proper wrench. The pains of separation treat me like the washerman who pounds a batch of laundry.

19 The nature of love is to confuse the bravest heroes. By day they search the mountains; they weep the whole night through. They sit there absorbed in thoughts of the beloved.

20 With their tongues everyone calls themselves a true friend. This part is easy, but when action is called for, one finds out what they are like.

21 Men's sincerity has changed and is no longer in keen demand. Everyone eats men's flesh now. Beloved, the fragrance of goodness will remain in this world. Others are just for show, there will be only one truly sincere man.

22 We give thanks for having found our dear friend while we lived. My lord, do not separate me from the one in whose company we found so much peace.

23 Having fixed your gaze, beloved, do not take it away. If you have taken it away, then fix it back again. Let the eyes maintain their habit forever. I have thousands of faults, but you should recognize the perfection in yourself, beloved.

Beloved, where did you learn your butchering? Take hold of a sharp knife, do not kill me with a blunt one. Look at all these wounds, the cuts inflicted by my sufferings. 24

Oh, now let him come, I wish my beloved would come. 25V
Taking the blind by the hand, he will deliver them to a safe place.
He will set this wretched girl's hut near to where he is.
He will lead the caravan safely through the mountain passes.
Mustafa will be our guide. He will deliver his people behind him.
Abdul Latif comes to say: Our friend will give us comfort.

25 Kapaiti

1 So long as you are spinning, do not turn your wheel by yourself. Otherwise, the dealer may spot a defect in this thread of yours.

2 Spin while you can, this opportunity is fleeting. Every spinner is approved according to the thread that they have spun. Those who know this properly do not let go of their ball of cotton.

3 This opportunity is fleeting, spin while you can. Turn your wheel and produce fine embroidery for your festive day. Otherwise, in the morning you may weep tears of blood with your friends.

4 You make no effort to spin, but stretch out your body to sleep. You will long to adorn yourself when your friends call you.

5 All you want to do today is relax, and you did not do any spinning yesterday. Your husband will show you no favors, you foolish girl.

6 All you want to do today is relax, and you did not do any spinning yesterday. Your spinning wheel's support posts have become detached, and its driving band has become slack. How wretched is the fate of those who have earned nothing from their spinning!

They sat about and wasted the days when they should have been spinning. You have not sat down by your wheel for a single moment, you foolish girl. How will you be able to hold your head high in the beloved's courtyard? 7

You have hands of gold, you perverse creature, why do you not spin? Sit in a corner and spin, and give up all this playing about. Then you may smile when you are called by the dealer, and get a better price. 8

Turn the broken wheel until the new one is fixed. You fool, do not let yourself fall into the bad habit of idleness. No one knows which girls will spin thread on the new wheel. 9

You wander about giving yourself airs, and this has made your husband furious. Sit down by the spinning wheel with your head modestly covered, so that your thread, though full of faults, may not go to waste. 10

Those who have spun fine thread with ill will in their hearts get none of it approved by the dealers. 11

Those who have spun coarse thread with love in their hearts sell it to the cotton dealers without its being weighed. 12

The spinners are filled with a love that makes them tremble while they spin. To make a profit, they 13 come early in the morning to the spinning place. The dealers are keen for their fine thread, says Shah. Their thread gets sold without being put on the scales and weighed.

14 The yarn of those who card it in secret is valuable. They do not let their hearts hear the sound of their wheel. Sitting in hiding, they tremble as they spin, says Latif. People offer them jewels for their thread, but they demand an even higher price.

15 Some wind yarn in Arabia, others spin in Kabul. Their thread is valuable and is exchanged for gems, but the all-powerful dealer does not reject the coarse thread that others spin.

16 You wander lost in pride; break that pride in pieces. It will make the thread you have produced worth nothing. Produce thread of decent quality here, you clumsy fool, where even those whose thread is far better shake and tremble.

17 The wheels are dismantled, and where have the spinners gone? The cotton balls of even the best girls lie around on the ground.

18 Yesterday they spun and spun, but they have not come into the spinning area today. The bands on their spinning wheels are slack, and their huts are closed.

Those cotton plants have gone, and so have the spinners. The bazaars seem desolate without them, and my heart is grieved. 19

As soon as they weighed the warp, many defects emerged. Summoning the spinner, they questioned her in secret. "I am so clumsy," she replied. "I could not straighten out the knots." 20

Take this to heart, you foolish woman, take this to heart. 21V
They carded a quarter of what had been carefully cleaned.
The birds have snatched your cotton balls, the wind has blown others away.
Dozing off beside your spinning wheel, you have enjoyed a sleep.
In the middle of the night, says Abdul Latif, wake and weep to delight the lord.

26 *Piribhati*

1 To keep his harp hanging on a hook is not the behavior of a bard. You are an enemy of the bright dawn. Who will call you a minstrel unless you practice your devotional art?

2 Why are you lying there fast asleep? Arise at dawn and weep. Tomorrow[1] your instrument will be left on the ground.

3 You sleep the whole night through, using your instrument as a pillow. Is this how a born minstrel will gain honor?

4 The title of true bard belongs to those who do not rest. With their instruments on their shoulders, they look for a path across the wilderness.

5 Minstrel, why do you roam in confusion? Where were you yesterday? Oh musician, give up this habit of wandering, says Latif. If you beg at the door of Sapar,[2] you will receive a fine reward.

6 The minstrel is weak, the way is long. Tell the son of Choto[3] to send me something here, since I cannot get there.

7 If accomplished musicians heard what he gives in secret to inexpert performers,[4] perhaps they would instantly destroy their instruments.

There are many singers there, why should they perform? Whatever task a man performs is always full of faults. You are the philosopher's stone, I am the iron. If you just glance at me, I am turned to gold. 8

Get up, you ignorant man, the call has come from Sapar. You may not have learned anything of singing, yet the king is pleased. "Beg from me," he says, "for I am yours." 9

Gifts are not bestowed according to caste; it is performance that is rewarded. The faults of the inexpert are tolerated by Prince Sapar. Anyone who spends the night with the king is freed from suffering. 10

Become ignorant and beg, forget all your knowledge. Last night Sapar prepared fine horses[5] for you. The lord of Las Bela is kind even to one who does not know how to sing. 11

You lie insensible, sleeping whole nights through. You do not get up in the middle of the night to spend time with Sapar. The descendant of Ronjho[6] opened his caskets in the night and took out pearls. The minstrels gathered to collect them and fill their pots. 12

The giver reproaches the minstrels on his own account. "Oh minstrel, why did you leave my 13 door and beg from others? That is why you have suffered days of hardship."

14 Oh minstrel, beg from the one who gives every day. The doors of the world are false, minstrel. If you beg from them, they will turn and reproach you tomorrow.

15 Prostrate yourself every day at the threshold of the giver. Oh minstrel, never remove your lips from it for an instant. Singers have no other opportunity besides singing.

16 Minstrel, do not forget Sapar for a moment. Fix your instrument and replace its strings with silver ones. Oh bard, go and utter your entreaties before him.

17 You are Sapar, I am a beggar. You are the master, I am the dog. I have put my instrument on my shoulder, in search of the way to you.

18 You are Sapar, I am a beggar. You are the master, I am sin. You are the philosopher's stone, I am iron; if you glance at me, I become gold.

19 The star has risen. Get up and offer the morning song of Vihag[7] to the bridegroom. Sapar is a jealous lord, he examines the hearts of the minstrels.

He gave great gifts and took the goods of the base. 20V
The lord bestowed presents of gold on fools.
The blind were bewitched, and he summoned the generous.
None of them realized, the lord did not take care of them.
You exalt whom you will and you bring low whom you will,[8] this is what happens to all there.
He favored the drop that is man, and made nothing of him.
He broke in turn all the cunning of the artful.
The envious are filled with sadness, and the false are led astray.
Sisters, says Abdul Latif, the lord is the one who pleases himself.

27 Sorath

1 Trusting in God, he departed from this place. The bard tied tassels and bells on his instrument. From afar he saw the palace of Rai Diyach. At that moment he made a supplication at the gate of God the one: "Oh gracious lord, grant that the king may be pleased with my music!"

2 He said to the king: "I have traveled here from a foreign land. You are of exalted rank, I am no expert, so how can I please you? This minstrel begs for your head.

3 Hearing of your glory, I have traveled here from a foreign land. I am utterly ignorant, what skill do I have in begging? Have a gift bestowed on me that will banish my desire.

4 I do not stay well in the cold, and in the heat I melt. Grant safety and protection to this beggar as he plays his instrument. Show the same favor to this beggar as God did to his friend.[1]

5 I have come to your door, oh king, as a minstrel who will take your life. Now save me from *the fire that burns.*[2] May God give you a place where there lies *the garden of Eden.*[3]

I have abandoned other doors and come to yours. 6
Spare a thought for me, oh handsome husband of Sorath. Good king, fill in turn the empty lap of this beggar."

A gifted minstrel came to Junagarh. That master 7
musician took out his instrument and sat down to play. The music its strings played caused a tumult throughout the city. The maidservants were confused, the ladies cried out. The minstrel made his instrument say: "This bard is a deadly hunter."

In supplication, Bijal loudly played his well-tuned 8
strings. The peerless king acceded to his request in his splendid chambers. In an auspicious moment the minstrel revealed a mystery to the king. The beggar called out: *I am Ahmad without the M.*[4] Only very few realized this, then both of them became one.

Only a very few men have some realization of this. 9
Those who have recognized this mystery have solved the riddle of *Man is my secret and I am his secret.*[5] That was what he told him; then the king and the minstrel became one.

The bard came from his home, thinking about the 10
king's head. He did not take bags of coins, and he rejected jewels, saying: "I have come to your door, since you have never learned to say no.

11 I am a hereditary minstrel," he said. The king replied: "Let me hear something from your heritage.

12 Sing me something, Bijal, and let me hear you, something that you sang to the accompaniment of your strings when you entered Girnar.[6] Will you return on your long journey, oh minstrel, or will you take your reward here?"

13 "I will take no reward at all, nor will I travel far. I have come bringing you a secret. Understand, oh husband of Sorath, that I will not return. Traveling from afar, I have come for you."

14 He asks for the head, he wants the head, without the head he cannot be content. He does not pass by the poor; he kills the leaders of the beautiful ones. He lays princes low and draws their life from them. Whether in the evening or in the morning, the creator will not spare anyone anywhere.

15 Bijal the bard sang something at dawn. In his apartments his royal majesty was pleased. "Come up, minstrel, and play before me. Let me sacrifice lakhs, says Latif, and place them at your feet. Come, guest, and I will give you this head.

16 Get in the palanquin, minstrel, and come up. The handsome king asks for you in his apartments.

Bijal, he promises to cut off his head for you at dawn."

The minstrel entered the palace with his magical instrument. When he touched the strings, fortresses fell down. Your fame spread, Bijal, and your song was heard everywhere. The handsome musician asked the king for his head. Junagarh became sad, and cries of mourning filled the balconies. 17

Just the generous king and the minstrel were there, with no one else between them. There was the same tune on the strings, the same idea in the minstrel's mind. Whether here or there, there was only this thought.[7] 18

"I offer you tenfold salutations, oh minstrel," said Diyach. "What you desire is not worth a single peppercorn. If you need my head, I will cut it off and give it to you twenty times over." 19

"I looked carefully on both sides of the forest," said the minstrel. "In my mind I considered those famous in different lands for their generosity. None but you promised their head." 20

"Minstrel, the one for whose head you bargained has no need of life. If you required something I did not have, it would have been a reproach to all donors in every age. 21

22 I sacrifice my head to you. Take this skull, minstrel, and depart quickly, lest you fail in your promise to Anirai.

23 I certainly do not consider my head to equal the music of your strings. This head has nothing worth offering, but do not return without my head, oh minstrel. There is nothing in this skull; as I take it off, I am ashamed.

24 If I put a hundred heads on the scales and weighed them against your strings, they would be outweighed by the side on which Bijal plays. My skull is an empty piece of bone, containing nothing worth offering.

25 If a million heads grew on mine, I would cut off each of them in turn a hundred times over. Even then the music of your strings would be worth more, oh minstrel."

26 "All are quite ready to cut off their heads and offer them,[8] oh Diyach. But the gift you give is the ultimate yardstick for beggars."

27 The singer was happy when he saw the prince's generosity. "Oh bard," said the king, "your recompense will be provided at dawn; my head is here right now. For true being lies in selflessness and nonexistence."

The minstrel made his way with his instrument on his 28
shoulder. On his way, says Shah, he cried out his
message. The generous and great-hearted king
was happy with him. Even Rai Diyach's mother
was happy.[9]

Bards do not enter palaces without some good end in 29
view. Bowing down, they see the light of divine
manifestation through their master's light.
Moonbeams shine in the frame of the handsome
king. His gifts, says Latif, are gained and are seen.
That is why rulers honor bards.

"Welcome, bard, I have understood your secret. We 30
have guessed the whole riddle that you tell. Be
happy with whatever is placed in your bowl.

Oh minstrel, what amazes me about your instrument 31
is that you survive safe when you strike the strings
with your hands. Last night you wounded my
heart with your harp."

The string does not play music but vibrates with the 32
sound of the divine mystery. Everyone says it is
the instrument that sounds, but it is the hands
of the player that make the music. Move swiftly
and become a falcon, then you will obtain the true
treasure.

33 I accept the message of your strings. My head is ready in exchange, but ask for something else. The body is something made of dust and clay; once it is cut up, it is nothing.

34 Oh bard, name something else, I will offer you whatever you want. My palace and my queen Sorath will not be enough if I weigh them against your strings. I have a secret; come near so that I may it tell it to you. Shall I cut off my head from my shoulders, minstrel, or shall I give it to you together with my body?

35 Three things have agreed with one another, the string, the knife, and the head. Bard, there is nothing better than the journey you have made here. Thanks and praise be to God that you asked for my head, oh minstrel."

36 The beautiful instrument played wonderful music. The great musician played in the king's presence without interruption. His essential light became apparent to Diyach. The sight made him take out his knife and stab it into his skull.

37 "The flower of Girnar has been plucked," the women of the city mourn. Thousands like Sorath arise and lament. They arrange the hair on the king's head and give it to the minstrel. The women lament and say: "Last night the king departed."

Sorath is dead,[10] there is peace, the prince has pitched his tents in heaven. There is music and that same fine display, as the strings play. Everywhere there is rejoicing, and see how the king is content. 38

Rai Diyach gave this head as a sacrifice to the lord. 39V
He departed from this place, leaving his queens and his kingdom.
He found favor before the gate of God. So many of his desires were fulfilled.
The minstrel obtained what he asked for by reciting to the accompaniment of his instrument.
Sisters, says Abdul Latif, his desires were amply fulfilled.

28 *Dahar*

1 Thorn tree, tell me stories of the lords of the old riverbed,[1] how they spent their nights and how they passed their days.

2 Thorn tree, if you were grieved for the lords of the old riverbed, there would be no blossom on your branches, and you would not put forth fresh shoots.

3 Thorn tree, what size were you when the old riverbed was in full flood? Have you met any travelers who are the equals of the Jasodhos?

4 In reality the old riverbed has dried up, and only *ak* bushes[2] grow on its banks. The brave traders have lost their strength, the water has dried up, and the tax collectors have gone.

5 The dried-up old riverbed has become a trickle, and reeds grow on its bank. The water has not returned in its former stream to the Patihal.[3] Only in a few spots do people gather.

6 The boatmen first realized that the old riverbed would not remain in its former state. Seeing how the water behaved, they turned their boats away. Brave companions like the Jasodhos fell prey to anxiety.

Oh great fish,[4] when there was a full flow of water you did not return. Why did you decide to come back later, when the water ebbed? Now you must suffer the attacks of the fishermen. 7

When there was plenty of water, oh great fish, you did not return. You will fall, today or tomorrow, into the fishermen's nets. 8

When the water was deep, oh great fish, you did not return. The fishermen have now blocked your passage with stakes. 9

You have become fat, oh great fish, and wildly you keep butting your way through. Now the time of that water in flood, which you once saw, is over. 10

When my beloved planted his hook in my gills, death did not strike me, but I felt the painful tug of the fishing line. 11

Oh lord of Medina,[5] hear my cries. Those who have fallen into deep water find refuge with you. Deliver them safely across. 12

Lord, send a wind that will blow me to my beloved. Let my heart not abandon hope on this well-traveled road. 13

14 My eyes looked for those camel riders, but they have not returned today. Without Prince Punhun,[6] they shed no tears.

15 As they watch, my eyes weep tears of blood. If the thought occurs to him, may Punhun take this wretched creature with him.

16 Today I clean my courtyard in hope of my beloved's return, after he has been away for so long in the mountains.

17 Your name is God, so I place great hope in you. Creator, there is no end or limit to your patience. Your name, lord, remains in my heart.

18 Lord, we have seen how wonderfully you demonstrate your authority. You make leaves sink to the bottom and stones float safely across. If you come to me, I will feel proud in spite of my unclean state.

19 Great is your name, and great is the mercy I beg you for. Without pillars or props, you are our shelter, you are our shade. What can I tell you? You know everything.

20 Oh veiler of sins, cover me, for I am naked. You who cover us, take me under the hem of your protection.

Oh husband, do pay a visit to this wretched woman's hut.[7] Beloved, the hem of your garment is my only protection. 21

While you remain present, husband, I am never sad. The roof of my hut leaks, and no one besides you knows how to fix it. 22

Others have many husbands; my husband is very forbearing. If his eyes see my faults, of his own accord he uses the edge of his garment to cover me. 23

You have been disagreeable to your husband but are merry with his foolish rival. You stupid woman with no sense, you leave the grain and gather the chaff. 24

Oh sleeping woman, arise and wake up, do not spend so long in slumber. You will not discover the joy of a royal marriage by sleeping. 25

Sleep for a while, wake for a while, do not spend so long in slumber. This place[8] you think is home is just somewhere for a midday nap. 26

Brother, those who have the distinction of staying awake remove the rust from their hearts, says Latif. Young man, make your resolution at dawn, says Shah. 27

28 These nights are few that you spend in delusion, you fool. There are many other nights to come for you to face alone.

29 Oh my girlfriends, sleeping has brought me much suffering. My sleep kept me from being close to my beloved.

30 The dawn has broken, night has gone, the constellations have grown dim. You fool, you will wring your hands over what you have lost.

31 Do not see what falls at dawn as dew, oh man. Night bursts into tears at the sight of those who suffer.

32 May the beloved not take his arm away or withdraw the edge of his garment at dawn. May I please my partner secretly from people.

33 The corrupted did not taste the milk but turned toward the froth. For the sake of this world they lost the world to come, and they were desolate.

34 Uttering their cries in the mountains, today they are about to depart. The cranes[9] create uproar in the desert plains at night.

35 Longing for its flock and remembering the lake, it experiences pain. As it pines, it sends messages to its beloved.

How did you forget your flock and come to sit here 36
in silent pining? Have you not been smitten by
thoughts of the beloved's sweet talk?

Yesterday your flock departed, oh crane. What will 37
you do on the lake without those you love?

They move in flocks, and their love for each other is 38
unbroken. See how birds show each other much
sweeter love than people.

Oh crane, be silent and do not stir up my wounded 39
heart with your cries. How long can those who
are smitten sit at home enduring the pain of
separation?

Yesterday the crane cried and made me think of 40
my beloved, without whom I spend my days in
sadness here.

Since yesterday the crane has been facing north and 41
singing sadly. She has seen her beloved in a dream,
and sings her songs at dawn.

The cranes are screaming; perhaps they are about to 42
go. Their children are left behind, and they depart
singing sadly.

To gather food for their young, the cranes have come 43
to the edge of the lake. The ground was hard for

them, and the birds hurt their feet when they landed.

44 The crane did not see the arrow that was trained in the mind of the hunter. Suddenly he took aim and scattered the flock.

45 Crane, you do not see the reeds with which the snare is covered. The hunter has killed thousands and scattered the flock.

46 Hunter, may you die and may your snare be destroyed. For yesterday you came between the lovers and separated them.

47 Mother, who can compete with the wealthy herdsmen[10] who leave such generous Thursday offerings?[11]

48 May those wealthy herdsmen enjoy a long life. I live under their protection. May they take care of us in difficult times.

49 If you want to go to green pastures, depart with the wealthy herdsmen. Then you will never hear laments of any loss.

50 The churning sticks can be heard as they go around in the pots. Travelers are welcome in the camps

of the wealthy herdsmen who give life to the destitute.

Wake up, Samos of the Jarejo tribe, do not lie there sleeping. See, Lakho[12] is approaching you and preparing to attack. 51

Their saddles are always tightly fastened, and their horses' coats are carefully brushed. These are the signs of bandits like Lakho. Tightening their horses' straps, they will create chaos in Kachchh. 52

Oh Rebari,[13] persuade Lakho with your pleas. Maybe the brave hero will turn away from attacking you. 53

Thousands of Lakhos are talked about, but none is the equal of Lakho Phulani. Princes and rajas tremble in their forts because of him. Even in their sleep the Jarejos do not lose their fear of him. 54

Lakho is mounted on his mare, Lakhi; Lakhi is Lakho's steed. He tightly girds his loins and carries off beautiful women. He will behave threateningly to everyone tomorrow. 55

They are all about to depart; none of them will stay, oh my friends. 56V
They will stay fixed here, all these beautiful places.
Those who possessed mighty kingdoms have departed in wretchedness.

Every soul shall have a taste of death[14] is the indication
to be understood.
The advocate will intercede there, he will caused
evildoers to be forgiven.
Oh God, says Abdul Latif, be merciful there, oh
coverer of faults.

29 *Bilaval*

Trust in these words: the giver has invited you. No sooner do you rinse your mouth[1] than he places food in it. 1

Do not drink the wine of heaven, but pass beyond it. Blessings that are bestowed on the way to union are extra gifts.[2] Everything is obtained in the presence of the Samo. 2

Oh Samo, the royal umbrella is raised over your head, though other men are turbaned.[3] You are a jewel; many people come to your abode. They receive alms to match their bowls. 3

The Samo calls those afflicted by great suffering. I become free from trouble as soon as he gets up and sets foot in his stirrups. Who besides you takes responsibility for those who seek refuge with you? 4

He is the support of the wretched, and takes responsibility for those who seek refuge with him. With thousands of supplicants before him, says Latif, the beloved does not hesitate. Where millions are struck dumb, his smile is plain to see. 5

Do not try to quench your thirst at every landing place; look toward the powerful spring. You will 6 receive thousands, says Latif, if you get to Rahu's kingdom. Behold the turban of the one who made the poor prosperous. He removes the rust from the hearts of millions, once he raises his head to speak.

7 Alauddin[4] came with a host of plumed warriors. No one dared to face him; who could endure his arrows? To save the honor of the Sumiro ladies, Abro mounted his camel. He was a brave leader, who was killed for the women's sake.

8 Providing comfort for those who sought refuge with him, the chieftain saved their honor. The Sumiro women who entered Abro's protection would not pay tribute.

9 All the others gave the women up, except for the ruler of the hills. He protected women he had not seen; how could he give up those whom he had seen? The chieftain turned many arrows aside.

10 Among the chiefs,[5] Abro is the greatest protector. The Samo forgot his own hunger for the sake of those who sought his protection. Jakhiro the chief is the support of those who look to him. He takes care of the weak and feeble.

11 Among the chiefs, Abro is like a mighty tree in the forest. No one has traveled the distance that hero

has trodden. Like the rains of Savan, the beloved makes the deserts fertile. The lord bestows a fine horse[6] on those who come to him just once.

Abro is most generous and kind, the best of all the Samos. Everyone comes to his door, and the lord of Kachchh does not turn his back on them. 12

God himself created Jakhiro and gave him form. Lifting his head like a lion, the hero twirls his moustaches. Like the ocean in flood, he drowns them in the deep water of his generosity. Mounted on his horse, the brave warrior guides those who travel on foot to the path. 13

Jakhiro truly deserves praise; all other rulers are like Anirai.[7] None of the others was formed like Jakhiro. Such was the clay from which he was formed. 14

Once you have seen Jadam Jakhiro, the others are all driven from your mind. So why dig wells once you have found a mighty spring? 15

No delay has to be endured at the hands of Jadam Jakhiro. Anyone who drinks near that Hatim[8] is filled. Let no one live in the world without that intoxicating wine. 16

17 No delay has to be endured at the hands of Jadam Jakhiro. "Come, welcome!" are the words in the mouth of the Samo.

18 I see no hero like Jakhiro in the land. He is the leader of all the prophets sent to the world; preeminent is his glory. He was granted the place of *There was the distance of two bow-lengths or less between them.*[9] It is the grace of the lord that he has brought me such a guide.

19 Why do you not bow down before Jakhiro, whose generosity has made the lands sated? The same people who trembled in rags are now wrapped in shawls. The Samo has filled all those who have begged from him.

20 God, may those heroes in whose protection I endure live long! May the well where travelers drink never dry up. Oh smiling lord, when my eyes behold you I am happy.

21 Coming to you, my thirst is quenched and my feet are cooled. Like a well in the wilderness, you take care of those who traverse the desert.

22 You are our protection, our veil, our refuge, our leader. Here your protection sustains us; in the next world our place is with you. No tribute is

paid by the destitute women who have taken refuge with Abro.[10]

When they see Jakhiro, minstrels are filled. To those who beg he gives a drop of heavenly wine. Their desire is quenched and they enter into union with him. 23

If he is transported today, he will rain drops of gold. The hero will make many full, Jakhiro will make the whole world full. 24

Vagand has returned, obtaining nothing through his schemes. Here he has obtained clothes, bread, and a fine place with the *pīr*.[11] 25

Vagand has returned from begging. He got a hard shoe beating, and nothing from his wife. He sits and says, "I will not go far from my *pīr*." 26

Vagand is sitting in expectation of his breakfast. He will never leave this spot, where he has smelled the fragrance of spring. 27

Vagand has keen expectations of his breakfast. He is weak in body but moves fast to eat. 28

Vagand has returned, smelling dirty and saying, "Dear lord, give me perfume, so that I may smell sweet." 29

30 Vagand has returned, foul and ugly. He does not put his smelly leather socks aside, but he is in love with the perfume seller.

31 Look at Vagand, sitting at the giver's door. He is sick but delights in being infected by his affliction.

32 Utterly infernal, Vagand has returned. Shah's heaven makes those who are dirty smell of roses. Discover rose perfume, so that you may always be fragrant.

33 Vagand has return, foul and failing to pray. Vagand falls on perfume like a hawk upon a partridge.

34 Ugly Vagand has returned from Kotri.[12] Hit him hard with a wooden stick.

35V He will cover me and will not leave me, my kind beloved who intercedes for me.
He will lead and accompany the blind, the foolish, and those who stumble.
He himself will give medicine for the unfortunate to drink.
He will cause sinners to pass through all difficult mountain paths.
Affirming the power of his divine light, Muhammad will accept their humble entreaties.
Everywhere he is their protector; in the future he will give them support.

The lord will give pure wine to those who are rejected.
Recognizing who he is, the perfect one will show his mercy.
Pitching his tent in the burning of the resurrection, he will set it up for sinners.
The generous one will avert the fate prescribed for sinners.
He will come at the time for help, and he will change the color of musk.
As *the mercy for the worlds,*[13] he will be our refuge from difficulty.
There the guide will take Abdul Latif by the hand.

30 Kedaro

1 The sight of the new moon of Muharram has made us concerned for the princes. The only one who knows is God, who does what he pleases.

2 Muharram has returned, but the Imams have not come. Oh lord, let me see the princes of Medina.

3 The princes went out from Medina, but they have not returned. Oh brother dyer, prepare black clothes. I am consumed with love for the royal travelers who have departed.

4 The harshness of martyrdom is all like the gentleness of the rains. Yazid has not the least understanding of this sign of love. The compact of being slaughtered was made with the Imams at the beginning of time.

5 The harshness of martyrdom is all a sign of the beloved's grace. Mystics understand the mystery of the business of Karbala.

6 The moon has set, and the brave princes have advanced from Medina with drums, hawks, axes, spears, daggers, and pikes. The brave sons of Ali will fight a battle with steel.

They have pitched their tents on the plain of Karbala. 7
They face Yazid and furiously engage in battle.
They do not turn their heads away from the
flashing swords.

The perfect members of the house of the Prophet 8
have come to Karbala. They wield swords of
Egyptian steel and fill the unbelievers with fear.
Such are the dear warriors to whom the lady
Fatima gave birth.

The perfect young heroes came to Karbala. The 9
earth shook and trembled, and there was uproar
in the heavens. This was not just a battle, but a
manifestation of God's love.

He lets his beloved friends be slain, and lets those he 10
loves be killed. He causes those who are especially
dear to him to suffer. *God the absolute*[1] has no
care, but does what he wishes. In all this there is
some profound mystery.

Did anyone see yesterday's battle of the warriors? The 11
elephants had their limbs cut off, and torrents of
blood flowed. They think the place where their
life is in danger is the best.

The armor polishers have come and burnished the 12
axes and swords. The heroes carry spears in their

hands and keep their weapons on their shoulders. Bravely they stand ready to face death.

13 In delight they strike blows, spur their horses, and take care of their companions. Unceasingly they wield the steel in battle.

14 The brave engage with the brave, and their swords clash. They hurl bodies upon bodies as they issue challenges and strike. They fall and their bodies writhe as the battlefield resounds with the tumult.

15 Here they challenge, and there they strike. Pipes and shawms are sounded on both sides. Horses and bridegrooms[2] engage with each other on the battlefield.

16 Horses and bridegrooms have only a few days to live. Once they were in palaces, now they are on the field of battle.

17 The dead bodies of the warriors come swaying in litters. Their wives throw handfuls of dust over themselves and shriek. They beat their breasts and lament as the battlefield resounds with the tumult.

18 “Oh my bridegroom,[3] come dressed in embroidered clothes for your wedding. Go quickly to the place where the spears are clashing. There is no need

to be afraid so long as the wedding rites have not been celebrated."

I will not say that he has run away, but I will believe it 19
if I hear he is dead. If my bridegroom has wounds on his face, I will rejoice. But I will die of shame if he has them on his back.

The women whose heads are held high now beat 20
themselves and utter laments. "Friends," they say, "these warriors have upheld the honor of their forebears."

"Bravo for your death, I weep for you. Do not come 21
back, my bridegroom. Taunts cast a long shadow, but life lasts only a little while."

There was dew on the ground and a breeze blew in the 22
air as night fell for the brave descendants of Ali in the battlefield.

Oh Yazid, cease to fight with the descendants of Ali. 23
You will not see the celebration[4] that will be held in honor of Lord Husain.

The Kufans did a terrible thing[5] and sided with Yazid. 24
The foul creatures attacked the hero on the battlefield. Their resolve was firm, and the lion attained martyrdom.

25 The Kufans wrote a letter, in which they swore by God: "We are your followers, you are our sovereign. Just come here, so that we may offer you the throne."

26 At Karbala, the Kufans do not let them drink water. Then the princes remember Lord Ali. They come out of their tents and look around, crying: "Come to our aid, oh Muhammad, Lord of Arabia."

27 At dawn a bird came swiftly from Karbala.[6] It arrived at the tomb of the Prophet and loudly cried: "I have seen the flashing of steel. Come to their aid, oh Muhammad, Lord of Arabia."

28 Hasan[7] was not with Husain, who had no helper or support. The princes' native land was far away. Is that why you attack so hard, Yazid?

29 Oh, if Hasan were in the army at the time of the battle, he would have been his close companion. He would have sacrificed himself like a moth for his brother. Who else is there to stop the attacks on Lord Husain?

30 Not all those who are present at the time of the battle are brave. Those who consider it disgraceful to turn back are the ones who fall on the field.

The warriors who put on armor at the time of the battle still have the desire to live. Those who fight unarmed deserve the name of hero. 31

Oh hero, if you would die for glory, then forget the idle fancies of your heart. Strike with the spear, engage at close quarters, and hold your shield straight. Strike with sword upon sword, so that you may prevail. 32

The brave Hur[8] advances quickly, saying: "Like a moth, I am a lover of the flame. May your grandfather the Prophet of God be happy with you. Oh bridegroom, let me sacrifice this revered head to you." 33

Hur received guidance from the beginning of eternity. He left the other side and entered the fray. As he came, he said to the Imam, "I sacrifice myself to you, in fulfillment of the words *God puts no burden on any person beyond his capacity*."[9] That bridegroom suffered wounds, and the brave hero became a martyr. 34

The hero stood in the field, wearing a helmet worth thousands. The perfect warrior wore a crest studded with jewels and gems. Lord Husain's turban was steeped in blood and gore. 35

36 His beard was dyed with blood, his teeth were as red as the pomegranate flower. His turban shone on the battlefield like the full moon. On the day when all are assembled before Muhammad, his mother will be pleased with him. Bravo for that hero, who was cut to pieces on the battlefield.

37 His mother wiped away the dust of Karbala. Ali wiped away the blood that flowed from his wounds. The creator forgave all sins in exchange for his blood.

38 So long as you live, oh prince who delights in battle, throw yourself on the points of the spears and drink the cup of steel. Make yourself food for the vultures who for years have sat waiting for it.

39 Vultures graze on the battlefield like goats on a hill pasture. Brave warriors engage with each other, racing to issue their challenges. The widows of the slain will cause a rise in the price of indigo.[10]

40 The heroic warriors who delight in battle do not hold back. The fighters sacrifice themselves for the sake of the Imams. The only task they perform is to fight *in the way of God.*[11] The houris in heaven garland the martyrs with flowers.

41 Heaven is the abode of those exalted heroes who proceed to paradise. Losing their separate

identity, they have become one with God. Lord, grant me the favor of seeing their faces.

Three groups wept for Hasan and Lord Husain: people in their homes, wild beasts in the jungle, and angels in the heavens. Birds beat their breasts in mourning for the dear one's departure. Oh God our true lord, grant the princes glory. 42

Those whose hearts contain no grief for Hasan and Lord Husain will never be forgiven by the creator, who is the omnipotent lord. 43

Alas, alas! The angels made their lament in the desert. 44V
Ah, ah! Lord Husain has departed.
On the plain of Karbala they pitched their tents.
He suffered his fate in accordance with God's will.
The lord has come to the plain of Karbala today.
Fate has caused the clouds to be filled with concern.
On seeing the harsh fate of Lord Husain, the prophets cried bitterly.
The angels wept, and heaven and earth trembled.
The sound of weeping fills the highest heaven.

ACKNOWLEDGMENTS

I am most grateful to Sheldon Pollock for his benevolent encouragement as general editor of the wonderful Murty Classical Library of India, to Leena Mitford and Marina Chellini for helping me with access to materials from the British Library, and to Dr. Fahmida Hussain for her help in getting books from the Sindhi Language Authority. This is also the place to record my gratitude to the late Ghulam Rabbani Agro, without whose past kindness over many years I should never have got to the point of embarking on this translation, and to Adriana Cloud of Harvard University Press, without whose hugely capable editorial expertise the book could never have been published in its present form.

NOTES

1 Kalyan

Kalyan is the name of a musical mode associated with the late evening or early morning, which is used to express devotional themes. This opening *sur* deals with core Sufi themes. The exceptional inclusion here of several *vāīs* is intended as a demonstration of the way *vāīs* are used to punctuate sequences of *abyāt* throughout the *Risālo.* The three sections (*dāstān*) of this *sur* are defined with unusual clarity by their subject matter. An explanation of the oneness of God and his creation (1.1–17V) is followed by descriptions of his lovers' readiness to suffer martyrdom (1.18–37V) and of the mixture of kindness and cruelty displayed by the divine beloved (1.38–53V).

1 Ar. *allāhu waḥdahu* (Qur'an 49.12).

2 Ar. *lā sharīka lahu* (Qur'an 6.163).

3 Ar. [*alā inna awliyā'a 'llāhi*] *lā khaufa 'alaihim wa-lāhum yaḥzanūn* (Qur'an 10.62) "[Behold, verily on the friends of God] there is no fear, nor shall they grieve."

4 Ar. *lā ilāha illā 'llāh* "there is no god but God," from the Islamic profession of faith.

5 The verse refers to the common conception of the four ascending stages on the Sufi path, in which the Law (Ar. *sharī'at*) is followed by the mystical Way (Ar. *tarīqat*), leading in turn to the higher levels of Reality (Ar. *haqīqat*) and Gnosis (Ar. *ma'rifat*). Compare 3.51, 7.32.

6 The recording angels Munkir and Nakir maintain a complete account of a person's life, which is presented to them at the moment of death.

7 Ar. *jalla jalālahu,* a phrase frequently added to a mention of God's name.

8 From which the whole of creation derives.

9 S. *mahesara* "great lord" is apparently a reference to the traditional association of the god Shiv with wine, but is here to be understood as the divine dispenser of spiritual wine, equivalent to the Pers. *pīr-e muġān* "the Magian elder."

10 Ar. *wa-tu'izzu man tashā'u wa-tudhillu man tashā'u* (Qur'an 3.26), addressed to God. Compare 26.20V.

11 Ar. *fa'dhkurūnī adhkurkum* (Qur'an 2.152).

12 Ar. *alastu bi-rabbikum* (Qur'an 7.172), the question addressed by

God to the unborn souls on the day of creation. See 7.63.

2 Yaman Kalyan

Yaman Kalyan is a musical variant of Kalyan. This long *sur* is similarly devoted to a series of core Sufi themes and images. The divine beloved is first addressed as the supreme doctor who alone has the power to cure the lover's sufferings (2.1–25). These sufferings are then described as a burning fire, and the beloved as a blacksmith in whose furnace the lover is plunged (2.26–41). A third set of verses then uses a familiar image of Persian poetry to speak of the lovers as drinkers of wine in the beloved's tavern (2.41–61). The core theme of the true practice of Sufism is then developed with particular reference to the teachings of the master Sufi Rumi (2.62–87). This leads to an evocation of the majesty of the divine beloved, the violence he inflicts on his lovers, and the patient fortitude they must practice (2.88–122).

1 A reference to the practice of a poet sharing the refreshments served to him with the singer who has performed his poetry.

2 Pers. *bar khez ba-dih sāqī,* a half-verse from a *ghazal* by the martyred Sufi saint Shah Inayat of Jhok. For another quotation from this poet, see 7.5.

3 The concluding phrase *illā'llāh* "except for God" in the Ar. phrase *lā ilāha illā'llāh* "there is no god but God," which is recited with inhalation and exhalation of the breath in the Sufi meditative exercise called *zikr.*

4 Ar. *sūfī lā kūfī* "the Sufi is not a Kufan," i.e., he is not bound by the teachings of the famous Kufan religious scholar Abu Hanifa (d. 767), the founder of the Hanafi school of Islamic law.

5 The reference is to the silent *zikr,* or internal repetition of the name of God, as opposed to the "spoken formula" of the next line.

6 This is the fundamental mystical understanding of the relationship between God and the universe that inspires the *Masnavī* of the great Persian Sufi poet Rumi (d. 1273).

7 The first letter of the Arabic alphabet and of the word *allāh,* also of the Qur'anic phrase *alastu bi-rabbikum* "am I not your lord?"; compare 1.47. The practitioners of formal religion fail to understand the spiritual significance of scripture.

8 Ar. *lā maqṣūda fī'l-dāraini [illā hū]* (Sufi saying).

9 One of the names of Satan.

10 Formerly an angel, Satan was cursed by God when he refused to

acknowledge the superior status of Adam. His apparent rebellion is explained by Sufis as a manifestation of his refusal to accept any authority besides God.

11 Meaning the primal covenant of the first day.

12 The compressed expression is not entirely clear.

13 When the letter *lām* (ل) is directly followed by *alif* (ا) it is written with the special digraph *lām-alif* (لا).

14 A demanding exercise of Sufi spiritual discipline.

15 The letter *alif* (ا), which also stands for the numeral 1.

16 The divine beloved is compared to David, the mighty king of Israel.

17 The biblical Cain (Ar. Qabil), who killed his brother Abel.

18 The original alliteration is between S. *sikaṇu* "desire" and S. *sūrī* "the gallows."

19 Ar. *muftī,* literally one who delivers fatwas, here standing for the voice of conscience.

20 Literally, those respond with the polite *jīu* "yes," rather than the rude *ḅauḍu* "yeah?"

3 Asa

Asa is a musical mode that is performed at dawn, and in most editions this *sur* is placed toward the end of the *Risālo.* But its contents are similar in character to those of the two opening *surs,* Kalyan and Yaman Kalyan. It is again devoted to the exposition of core Sufi teachings, beginning with the mystery of existence (3.1–8), before developing the theme of the need for eyes to see the beauty of the divine beloved (3.9–30). The later verses of the *sur* (3.31–56) emphasize the need for absolute sincerity and single-mindedness in the mystical quest, and the requirement to get rid of the self if one is to attain the necessary clarity of vision.

1 Ar. *inna 'llāha witrun yuḥibbu 'l-witra* (Hadith), referring to the unity of God. The "odd number" is one.

2 Creation, as opposed to God.

3 Ar. *al-insānu sirrī wa-anā sirruhu* (Hadith). Compare 27.9.

4 Ar. *fānī fī 'llāhi.*

5 This recalls the story of people touching different parts of an elephant in a darkened room and trying to work out what it was, which is told in Rumi's *Masnavī* (3: 1259–1266).

6 There is wordplay between Ar. *fī'l-ḥaqīqat* "in reality" and *fīl* "elephant."

7 Ar. *lam yalid wa-lam yūlad* (Qur'an 112.3). Compare 15.61, 16.24.

8 The father of Ibrahim, who was a fanatical idol worshiper.
9 Ar. *ashhadu,* from the Islamic profession of faith.
10 The claim of possessing true identity can be properly made only by God.
11 See 1.5 for the four stages of the Sufi path.
12 Ar. *alladhīna āmanū wa-kānū yattaqūna* (Qur'an 12.57).
13 Ar. *waḥdahu lā sharīka lahu* (Qur'an 6.163); see 1.2.
14 Ar. *inna auliyāī taḥta qabāī* (Hadith).
15 Ar. *lā ya'rifuhum ghairī* (Hadith).

4 *Khambhat*

Khanbat is the name both of a musical mode and of a city in Gujarat (compare 22.34), which was formerly known in English as Cambay. The *sur* falls into two parts. In the first part (4.1–18) the beauty of the distant beloved is said to outshine even the moon, which is asked to take the lover's message to him. In the second part (4.19–40V) the lover asks his camel to take him to the beloved, while also bewailing its disobedience and bad habits of preferring coarse desert plants to the fragrant sandal. As elsewhere, the greedy camel here personifies the lower self (Ar. *nafs*) with its stubborn resistance to the spiritual life.

1 A common desert shrub.
2 A desert plant with poisonous milky juice.
3 Camels are harnessed to turn the circular presses used to crush oil seeds.
4 A fragrant plant.
5 A variety of sandal.

5 *Sirirag*

Sirirag (Skt. *Śrīrāga-*) is the name of a well-known Indian musical mode. This *sur* uses the imagery of the sea voyages undertaken by the traders of Sindh as a symbol for human life. Constant vigilance is enjoined as the only means of ensuring against the numerous dangers that beset the traveler, if he is safely to bring home the treasure he seeks.

1 I.e., wearing diving masks.
2 A port in Gujarat, here symbolizing the destination of life's journey.
3 Portuguese pirates had an evil reputation in the seas around Sindh.
4 The port in Yemen that was a regular destination for traders from Sindh.

5 This is a riddling verse variously explained by different editors.

6 The devil.

7 Like Suhini, who bravely entered the water without an earthen pot as a float. Compare 7 below.

8 Ar. *kullu nafsin dhā'iqatu 'l-mauti* (Qur'an 3.185, 29.57). Compare 14.64V, 28.56V.

9 Ar. *yauma yafirru 'l-mar'u min akhīhi* (Qur'an 80.34), describing the signs of the last day.

10 The word refers to a well-known Hadith: Ar. *al-dunyā jīfatun ṭālibuhā kilābun* "the world is a piece of carrion that is sought after by dogs."

6 Samundi

Like the preceding *sur*, this one (S. *sāmūṇḍī* "sailor") is based on the theme of traders sailing away on voyages for business. But here the mood is lyrical rather than didactic, and the emphasis is upon the suffering of the wives who have been parted from their beloved husbands.

1 As in several of the following verses, the quotation marks indicate the words of the woman who has been left behind.

2 The bird that brings messages from the beloved.

3 It was the custom for the wives of the Hindu traders of Sindh to make offerings to the water deity for their husbands' safe return.

4 The making of a vow is marked by lighting lamps and by tying ribbons on trees.

5 With her husband away on a winter voyage, the woman is left behind to face the hardships of the season on her own.

6 Famous for its wealth, which attracted sailors from distant Sindh.

7 The Hindu festival of lamps celebrated in the autumn, which marked the beginning of the trading season.

7 Suhini

This long *sur* is devoted to the sufferings of Suhini, the heroine of a very popular local romantic legend (Shackle 2022: 388-400.). The Sindhi version, which is rather different from the Panjabi story cited in most modern descriptions, is set among the pastoral tribes who grazed their buffaloes in the pastures watered by the Indus. As in so many traditional romances, there is a tension between Suhini's conventional duties as a woman whose marriage to her husband, Dam, has been arranged by their families and her passion for Sahar, a prosperous herdsman from another tribe. This was first ignited when Sahar, also called Mehar, literally "buffalo herdsman," unwittingly gave her a cup of milk infused by a saint with the magical power to inspire love. Unable to resist her passion, Suhini regularly crosses the Indus to see her beloved, using an earthen pot as a float, until a member of her husband's family finds out and substitutes an unfired pot. Braving a winter storm, Suhini sets out that night as usual only to discover in midstream that her float is useless. Surrounded by the cruel creatures of the deep, she drowns in the raging waters of the Indus, where she is lamented by her beloved.

The verses of the *sur* dwell at length upon Suhini's sufferings on this final journey from the moment when she bravely plunges into the river to her tragic end. As always in the *Risālo*, there is a wealth of vivid concrete detail in the descriptions of the great river, while the spiritual allegory is constantly present. Suhini's courage is upheld as an example to all true seekers of the divine, as opposed to the insincere who rely on mechanical aids to cross the river. The divine beloved is symbolized by Sahar, who can only be reached on the far bank after much struggle, while the vast river that is itself comparable to a sea symbolizes the ocean of existence that every soul must traverse without falling prey to its dangers and delusions.

1 Pers. *sar dar qadam-e yār fidā shud chi ba-jā shud*, a verse from a poem by the famous Sindhi Sufi martyr Shah Inayat of Jhok (d. 1718). This is one of the very few Persian quotations in the *Risālo*, but compare 2.49.

2 The full sense of Ar. *wa ammā man khāfa maqāma rabbihi* (Qur'an 55.45) is "but for such as fear the time when they will stand before the Judgment Seat of their Lord."

3 Ar. *ṭālibu 'l-maulā mudhakkaru* (Sufi saying).

4 Ar. *lā taqnaṭū min raḥmati 'llāhi* (Qur'an 39.53). Compare 11.42V.

5 S. *toḍ̤ī* "beautiful" is an exact synonym and alternate name for Suhini.

6 That is to say, God, the universal beloved.

7 See 1.5 for the four stages on the Sufi path.

8 The reference is to the cup of enchanted milk that first made Suhini fall in love with Mehar. Compare 7.56.

9 A common idiom, meaning "may no harm befall him."

10 Temporary alluvial islands (S. *b̤eṭu*) are regularly formed in the middle of the river.

11 See 7.44.

12 The phrase "Let it be, and it was" comes from the end of the Arabic verse [*badīʿu 'l-samāwāti wa 'l-arḍi wa idhā qaḍā amran fa-innamā yaqūlu lahu*] *kun fa-yakūnu* (Qur'an 2.117), "[The creator of the heavens and earth, and when he decrees a thing he but says to it,] 'Let it be,' and it is." The expression is frequently used by the Sufi poets to refer to the act of creation, so here it indicates how the lovers were intended for each other from pre-eternity, even before the moment of creation. Compare 15.2.

13 The primal covenant, formed at the time of creation, between God and man is commonly evoked in the scriptural verse *alastu bi-rabbikum qālū balā* [*shahidnā*] (Qur'an 7.172) "'Am I not your lord?' They said, 'Yes, [we so testify].'" Compare 1.47, 15.1.

14 In this famous line, Shah Latif claims for his poems (S. *baita*) a status comparable to the verses of the Qur'an (S. *āyatūn̤*).

15 After death, the soul will be held to account for the record of its previous life that has been maintained by the angels Munkir and Nakir. See 1.6, 8.72.

16 That is, the self-proclamation of identity with the divine famously expressed in the Arabic phrase *anā 'l-ḥaqq* "I am God," which was uttered by the great Sufi martyr Mansur. The oblique reference to this notorious expression, so frequently invoked by other Sufi poets like Bullhe Shah and Sachal Sarmast, is a telling illustration of Shah Latif's preference for the indirect expression of a profoundly Sufi understanding of the world.

17 The phrase "milk drinker" (S. *khīra-piyāka*) suggests the purity as well as the occupation of the buffalo herder Mehar.

18 This long *vāī* is one of the finest examples of the genre in the *Risālo*. There is a tradition that it was Shah Latif's final composition, and this is reflected in its placement at the end of the entire *Risālo* in Kazi 1961; compare Baloch 2012. The unusual rhyme *-āba* involves the use of numerous Arabic loanwords, which in turn generate some unusual images as the successive verses of the poem offer a loose series of instructions for a life informed by mystical understanding.

19 The rebab stands for the joys of music and pleasure, as opposed to the austerities of the pious life.

20 This is variously interpreted to indicate the mystery of humility, or the special character of man, formed from clay.

21 The "thief" is the lower self (Ar. *nafs*), to whose destruction the Sufi life is dedicated.

22 The parallel is drawn from the technical language of Arabic

linguistics. The final short vowels marking inflection (Ar. *iʿrāb*, here the rhyme word) are in some cases regularly subject to assimilation (Ar. *idghām*), as when the rule forbidding a sequence of four or more short vowels in successive syllables results in the joining of consonants, so that, e.g., Ar. *jaʿala laka* becomes *jaʿallaka*.

8 Sasui Abiri

This *sur* (S. *sasuī ābirī* "Sasui the weak") is the first of five based on the very popular tragic romance of Sasui and Punhun. Compare Shackle 1985 for a complete translation of the later Panjabi narrative poem *Sassī Punnūṉ* by Hasham Shah.

As usual, however, Shah Latif alludes only in passing to earlier parts of the story. Sasui was originally a Brahman's daughter, but when a prophecy warned her father that she would bring disgrace on the family she was abandoned and brought up by a washerman in the city of Bhambhor. The fame of her beauty attracted Punhun, the prince of a Baloch tribe, whose father, Ari Jam, was the ruler of Kech in Balochistan. (Punhun is frequently referred to by his tribal name, Hôt, which is here spelled with a circumflex accent over the long vowel to distinguish it from the common English word "hot.") Punhun came with his brothers on a trading expedition to Bhambhor, where Sasui fell in love with him. She passed him off as a member of her caste by slipping gold coins into the clothes he was unable to wash properly, and in this way secured her foster father's permission for their marriage. But Punhun's brothers were strongly against a mere washergirl marrying the son of their tribal chief. Using the wedding celebrations to get Punhun drunk, they abducted him from Sasui's side while the couple slept. Putting him on a camel, they raced back to Kech.

This turning point marks the story's tragic conclusion, which is the main focus of Shah Latif's treatment in this and the following *surs*. Sasui wakes up to find herself abandoned. Utterly distraught, she races out into the wilderness in search of Punhun. Her route from Bhambhor toward Kech in Balochistan leads across the barren territory of Las Bela, across the Pab and Harho hills, through the wooded area of the Vankar, and over the Hab and Vindar rivers. Her thoughts are entirely obsessed with her distant beloved, whose memory is evoked by a variety of epithets, including the tribal name Hôt and his patronymic Ari. Just before her death from heat and exhaustion Sasui comes across a lone shepherd. When she dies, still without having managed to track down her beloved, the shepherd digs the grave in which Punhun will also be buried when he eventually comes in search of her.

The story is thus a counterpart to the tale of Suhini, with the death of the heroine taking place in the desert rather than the Indus, but similarly serving in the *Risālo* as a powerful image for the devoted pursuit of the divine beloved.

1 A direct reminiscence of a verse from Rumi's *Masnavī*: Pers. *tishnagān gar āb joyand dar jahān, āb ham joyad ba-ʿālam tishnagān.*

2 Sasui, who was born a Brahman.

3 The verse explains the mystical secret of true love, in which the lover realizes their true identity only when their false sense of self has been destroyed by the sufferings inflicted by their love.

4 A name of the devil, here with the sense of "do not be led by the lower self."

5 A range of mountains in Las Bela, lying on the route from Bhambhor to Kech.

6 The people of Kech, i.e., those who had taken Punhun.

7 A wooded area in Las Bela.

8 S. *kohiyāru*, i.e., Punhun.

9 A river in Las Bela flowing from the Pab range down to the sea.

10 Yogis wear ochre-colored clothes and have their ears split to accommodate their large earrings.

11 Sasui blames herself for not entertaining Punhun's brothers in the way that a proper wife should.

12 I.e., Sasui, who belonged to the washerman caste (S. *parīṭi*) but was born a Brahman.

13 The last line is addressed to God. Since he is omnipresent, why should the Sufis who reveal this be condemned?

14 Ar. *khalaqa ādama ʿalā ṣūratihi* (Hadith).

15 As often, Bhambhor symbolizes this world.

16 Ar. *mā ra'aitu shai'an illā wa-ra'aitu 'llāha* (Sufi saying).

17 Ar. *wa-fī anfusikum afalā tabṣirūna* (Qur'an 12.51).

18 Ar. *wa-naḥnu aqrabu ilaihi min ḥabli 'l-warīdi* (Qur'an 50.16).

19 Ar. *allāhu bi-kulli shai'in muḥīṭu* (Qur'an 4.162).

20 A river that flows from the Pab hills down to the sea.

21 The angel of death, who appears to those about to die.

22 The two angels who record a person's every action throughout their life and present them with their account at the moment of death. Compare 1.6, 7.79.

23 The seemingly contrary advice points to the impossible pain of the journey of love. Compare 8.76.

24 The yogis (S. *khāhoṛī*) who live on whatever they can find in the wilderness. See 19.

9 Ma'zuri

The second of the Sasui *surs* (S. *ma'zūrī* "helpless, handicapped."). See 8.

1 Compare 8.8.

2 An imagined pet name for the beloved's dog.

3 See 8.40.

4 See 13.

5 This verse and those following emphasize the detachment of the beloved from worldly existence and the need for those who love him to become similarly detached.

6 Sasui threatens the trees if they do not help her get to Punhun.

7 A translation of the well-known Sufi tradition Ar. *mūtū qabl an tamūtū*. Compare 9.29.

8 Ar. *mūtū [qabl an tamūtū]* "Die [before your death]." See 9.24.

9 I.e., she has staked everything on immediate action.

10 A direct reminiscence of the opening verse of Rumi's *Masnavī*; see 24.2.

11 In order to catch a glimpse of Punhun's company in the distance.

12 The Indian cuckoo, whose mournful cry is regularly associated in Indian poetry with the sound of a lover's lament.

10 Desi

The third of the Sasui *surs*. See 8. Desi is the name of a well-known musical mode.

1 Ar. *al-safaru qiṭ'atun min al-nāri* (Hadith).

2 Ar. *sirāṭa 'l-mustaqīma* (Qur'an 1.5).

3 See 7.62.

4 Ar. *man ṭalaba shai'an wa-jadda wajada.*

5 Ar. *man lā shaikhun lahu fa-shaikhuhu 'l-shaiṭānu* (Sufi saying).

6 Ar. *bilā shaikhin yamshī fī 'l-ṭarīqi [ka-man yamshī fī 'l-baḥri bilā safīnatin]* (Sufi saying).

7 S. *pārīsī*, i.e., Balochi, the semi-Persian argot of the camel-herding tribes (S. *jata*).

8 Daulat, literally "Prosperity," the kind of name given to a slave girl.

9 I.e., after Sasui's death, when Punhun eventually found her.

10 Here Sasui expresses her extreme humility.

11 I.e., the two menacing hills that lie on her path are easy to get through.

12 Epithet of Punhun.

13 I.e., those who have not learned to detach themselves.

14 Here the reference is to the prophet Muhammad in his role as intercessor on the day of judgment.

15 The tribe of camel drivers. Compare 10.17.

11 Kohiyari

The fourth of the Sasui *surs*. See 8. S. *kohiyārī* "mountain dweller" indicates the particular focus of this *sur* (particularly 11.8–36) on the sufferings of Sasui as she journeys through the mountains.

1 Verses 11.1–2, reproaching Sasui for sleeping while Punhun was taken away, are macaronics that include several Arabic words besides this longer phrase.

2 A reference to Ar. *a-lam naj'ali 'l-arḍa mihdan, wa 'l-jibāla awtādan* (Qur'an 78.6–7). "Have we not made the earth as a wide expanse, and the mountains as pegs?"

3 The shepherd whom Sasui encountered at the end of her journey through the wilderness.

4 Used as a fixative in dyeing cloth.

5 Ar. *lā taqnaṭū min raḥmati 'llāhi* (Qur'an 39.53). See 7.11.

6 Ar. *inna 'llāha yaġhfiru 'l-dhanūba jamī'an* (Qur'an 39.53).

12 Husaini

The fifth Sasui *sur*. See 8. Consisting of a large number of generally short verses, this *sur* is notable for the pathos with which it evokes the sufferings of Sasui as she goes in quest of Punhun. It is set to the musical mode Husaini, which is associated with laments for the martyrdom of Imam Husain at Karbala; see introductory note to 30. The mode is mentioned in the text at 12.38 and 12.96.

1 Compare 10.17.

2 See 8.8.

3 I.e., that she belonged to the lowly washerman caste.

4 Name of a river in Las Bela.

5 See introductory note above, and compare 12.96.

6 Love is paradoxically felt most keenly when the lovers are apart.

7 I.e., the sufferings that are actually the joys given by love.

8 Who sprinkles hot iron with water in order to cool it down as he beats it.

9 This verse is supposed to be a response by Shah Latif to his father's appeal in 12.75.

10 The mountain passes reply to Sasui's question.

11 When Punhun died after finding Sasui's corpse, the lovers were buried together.

12 Fatima, the mother of Husain. Compare 12.38.

13 Lila Chanesar

The *sur* relates to the unusual legend of the Rajput ruler Chanesar, also called Dasaro; his queen, Lila; and the princess Kaunru, who made plans with her mother to win Chanesar for herself. Knowing Lila's fondness for jewelry, Kaunru showed her a fabulously valuable necklace, which she promised to give her in exchange for being allowed to spend one night with Chanesar. But when Chanesar discovered how he had been tricked, Lila lost both her husband's love and her status as his queen. Most of the *sur* deals with Lila's laments for her lost fortune or condemnations of her foolish betrayal of love for material gain. Through the tacit equation of Chanesar with God, the theme of the divine jealousy of rival objects of worship is also developed.

1 Literally, "Chanesar is four-colored, the rest of the world is two-colored."

2 The reference is to a wedding ritual, in which it was believed to be unlucky if the groom's feet were not placed straight upon the bride's when he entered her parental home.

3 A symbol of her former life of luxury as Chanesar's queen.

4 Kaunru and her mother, who came to Chanesar's palace in pursuit of the plan for her to seduce him.

14 Mumal Rano

The *sur* is based on incidents from the legend that describes the love between Mumal, a beautiful princess from the Gujar tribe, and Mendhiro, a Sodho Rajput usually referred to by his royal title, Rano. Mumal lived in the magical palace of Kak on the banks of the river Ludano, where she used to lure lovers to their death. When Rano succeeded in overcoming her enchantments, Mumal fell in love with him. To arouse his jealousy, she played a trick on him, but he believed she had been unfaithful and abandoned her. Mumal then became distraught without him and begged him to return.

1 The opening section of the *sur* (14.1–16) evokes the meeting between Rano and his friends on their way to Kak and a former suitor of Mumal whose suffering for the sake of her love has made him become a yogi.

2 By his description of Mumal.

3 Rano and his three companions.

4 According to the story, this action destroyed the enchantment that had been placed over Kak.

5 This refers to an incident in the story, when Mumal set out to arouse Rano's jealousy by sleeping with her sister Sumal dressed as a man.

6 When Rano found the sisters in bed together, he furiously left his staff behind to show Mumal that he had been there.

7 To discover which one had been sleeping with Mumal.

8 The shameless are imagined to have a whole set of artificial clay noses, so it does not matter to them if one is cut off.

9 A royal title.

10 Ar. *kullu nafsin dhā'iqatu'l-mauti* (Qur'an 3.185, 29.57). Compare 5.67V, 28.56V.

15 Marui

The *sur* is based around the story of Marui, who was born into the Maru tribe of nomads living in Malir, in the Dhat area of the Thar desert to the east of Sindh. Marui had been betrothed to a fellow tribesman, here referred to simply as "the Maru," rather than by his given name, Khetsen. But reports of her beauty attracted the attention of Umar, a local Rajput chieftain, who one day abducted her and imprisoned her in his fortress of Umarkot. Most of the *sur* describes how Marui resisted his demands and the temptations of palace life, thinking only of her Maru and longing to return to the simple life of the desert. In allegorical terms, it thus dwells on the central tension in human life between the recollection of man's original condition of being at one with the divine and the contrary lures of the lower self toward the luxuries of this world. The *sur* also allows for a nativist interpretation that exalts the authenticity of the values and landscape of Sindh.

1 Ar. *alastu bi-rabbikum, qālū balā* (Qur'an 7.172). See 7.63.

2 Ar. *kun fa-yakūnu* (Qur'an 2.117). See 7.62.

3 Ar. *qaidu 'l-mā'i*, i.e., the power of fate. The full form of the saying

is Ar. *qaidu 'l-mā'i ashaddu min qaidi 'l-ḥadīdi* "the prison of water is mightier than the prison of iron."

4 Ar. *hanā ka-jismī wa 'l-fu'ādu ladaikum*, a popular phrase.

5 Ar. *jaffa 'l-qalamu bi-mā huwa kā'inun* (Hadith).

6 I.e., Marui and her beloved.

7 Ar. *bakati 'l-'ainānī fī hawāka damman*, from a poem. The many Arabic quotations in this section suggest a parallel between the Marus (here actually called S. *i'rābiyuni*) and the noble Bedouin of Arabia.

8 Ar. *kullu shai'in yarji'u ilā aṣlihi*, a common phrase.

9 The natural dye used by the nomads to color their clothes.

10 For the Eid festival.

11 Ar. *qul lan yuṣībanā illā mā kataba 'llāhu* (Qur'an 9.51).

12 A simple dish made from desert plants, as opposed to the richness of pulao, made from meat and rice.

13 See 15.1.

14 See 3.32.

15 Ar. *laisa ka-mithlihi shai'un* (Qur'an 41.11).

16 When the well is monopolized by men and their animals.

17 Marui here refers to her abduction by Umar.

18 Compare 22.5.

19 According to popular belief, the oyster does not drink water from the ocean or river where it lives. It waits instead for clouds to appear in the sky, when it opens to drink the raindrops that it lives on.

20 Pearls are thought to be produced by the hunger and thirst the oyster suffers in the sea.

21 The spinning place (S. *ātaṇu*) is where the young women gather to spin and enjoy each other's company.

22 The speaker here is the poet himself.

16 Kamod

Kamod is a musical mode associated with feelings of joy. The *sur* celebrates the love shown by the Samo ruler Tamachi to the fishergirl Nuri, whose home was by the Kinjhar lake. The various castes of fishermen, named in the *sur* as Gandiri, Mangar, Me, and Muhano, were traditionally ranked as the lowest of the low in Sindhi society, but Tamachi's favor promotes Nuri above his royal queens. The parallel is with the divine favor that may be enjoyed by all sinners, no matter how full of faults they may be.

1 Literally, "made the Me girl a full human being" (S. *māṛihū kayo me*).
2 Meaning that the ladies of the court have no social interaction with the humble circles in which Nuri moves.
3 Ar. *lam yalid wa-lam yūlad* (Qur'an 112.3).

17 Ghatu

This very short *sur* deals with the fate of a family of expert fishermen (S. *ghātū*). It is loosely related to a local legend that describes how the six brothers of the fisherman Moriro were killed by a monstrous crocodile that lived in the whirlpool of Kalachi (near the site of modern Karachi), and how Moriro then contrived the monster's destruction. The story naturally lends itself to interpretation as an allegory of the struggle against the power of the lower self; several verses of the *sur* are also devoted to the lyrical theme of lament for the death of the fishermen in the whirlpool.
1 This and the following verses are to be understood as laments by one of the dead fishermen's wives.
2 The verse pictures the collapse of the local fish market, including the fishmongers and the tax collectors, following the loss of the fishermen.
3 In order to carry on dealing with the fishmongers in the market.

18 Ramakali

This lengthy *sur* praises the various groups of Hindu yogis who wandered from one place to another in Sindh or beyond as ideal practitioners of the spiritual life. They are praised for their unwavering focus on the divine and for their resolute refusal of all worldly comforts. See further the illuminating study of this *sur* in Schimmel 1976: 219–235.
1 The pairing is to be understood as analogous to the familiar Sufi division between devotees of divine beauty (Ar. *jalālī*) and those of divine majesty (Ar. *jamālī*).
2 This final phrase is repeated throughout 18.1–16.
3 The small animal horn (S. *siṅī*), which is the characteristic instrument of the yogis. Compare 18.118V.
4 This seems to be the meaning of this highly condensed half-line.
5 The homeland of the yogis is regularly said to lie east, i.e., in the Gangetic valley where so many of the sacred sites of Hinduism are located.

6 A stringed instrument played with a bow, somewhat similar to the *sārangī*.
7 S. *lāhūtī* from Ar. *lāhūt* "divinity" is a common epithet of the yogis in this *sur*. It is sometimes understood as "Lahuti," meaning either a member of a particular sect of yogis or coming from Lahut, the name of a small place in Sindh on the yogis' pilgrimage route.
8 A remote site in Balochistan, sacred to the goddess (S. *nānī*), and an important center of pilgrimage for the yogis.
9 A city in Gujarat, closely associated with Krishna. But Shiv is the god to whom most yogis are particularly devoted; compare 18.65.
10 Ali, the nephew of the Prophet, is regarded as a spiritual authority by many Sufis. The multiple religious references in this verse are remarkable for their blurring of conventional boundaries.
11 This opening formula is developed as a cycle of twelve days throughout 18.17–28.
12 Here used as the common Hindu name for God, although yogis are characteristically associated with Shiv.
13 The "split-ear" order of yogis whose initiation involves splitting the cartilage of the ear in order to insert the large wooden rings by which they are distinguished.
14 Another remote destination that the yogis make pilgrimage to.
15 I.e., it pierces me like a thorn when I see that it is empty.
16 This phrase introduces another set of verses, 18.35–39.
17 Compare 18.4.
18 Compare 18.14.
19 I.e., "putting their head on their knees, they have a vision of the divine presence." Mount Sinai is where God revealed himself to Moses. In popular iconography, Shah Latif is often depicted in the yogic posture of sitting with his head supported by his knees.
20 The niche in the wall of a mosque marking the direction of Mecca toward which worshipers offer prayer.
21 The divine beloved is everywhere, no matter which direction one faces.
22 As elsewhere, Shah Latif's description of the yogis' freedom from narrow religious constraints moves naturally from a Hindu to an Islamic frame of reference.
23 Compare 18.33.
24 I.e., the ritual ablution (S. *vuzū*) performed before the Muslim prayers.
25 Instead of the Arabic call to prayer (S. *bāngu*) they hear the

pre-Islamic sound of the sacred Hindu syllable (Skt. *oṃ*).

26 The master revered by most orders of yogis.

27 The opening phrase (S. *aju na otāqani men*) is repeated in verses 18.84–87, which form a set.

28 The final phrase (S. *lāhūtī laḍ̤ī viyā*) is repeated in 18.85–86.

29 From the bonfires that yogis light wherever they stay.

30 To the place of the beloved.

31 The hill in District Hyderabad in southern Sindh that marks the starting point of the pilgrimage to Hinglaj.

32 I.e., become willing to die before their death, as enjoined in the Sufi phrase Ar. *mūtū qabl an tamūtū* "die before you die." See 9.24, 9.29.

33 I.e., the darkness of this world.

34 The exact opposite of 18.113. For another example of paired negative and positive verses, compare 18.114–115.

35 Literally, "what has passed and what passes," i.e., material possessions.

36 Ali's rejection of worldly goods is captured in the saying Ar. *al-faqaru fak̤hrī* "poverty is my pride."

37 Here the sense seems to be that merely holding a horn is not necessarily a sign of the true yogi.

38 Cotton quilts (S. *ruliyūṇ*) are associated with the poor.

39 This fine *vāī* in praise of the yogi's horn contrasts it with the inferior qualities of the various instruments mentioned in other *surs* of the *Risālo*.

40 Apparently referring to the double shawm (S. *murilī*), a wind instrument constructed with a gourd.

41 Compare 7.38, 7.41.

42 See 27.

43 Hind denotes the Gangetic region, as opposed to Sindh and the Indus valley.

19 Khahori

Khahori (S. *khāhoṛī* "forager") refers to the yogis who roamed the wilderness gathering the vegetation that was their sole diet. Gathered with great difficulty, these wild plants in turn symbolize spiritual knowledge that is to be gleaned only with a comparable effort. Like the preceding *sur*, this one describes the yogis as supreme practitioners of the spiritual life.

1 The mantras that the yogis utter.

2 Literally, "became Lahutis" (S. *lāhūtī thiā*), meaning those who have become part of the divine world (Ar. *lāhūt*). Compare 18.10.

3 A burning bonfire is the sign of a yogi's camping place.

20 Purab

This *sur* falls into two distinct parts. The opening verses (20.1–14) are based on the familiar theme of Indian poetry in which the crow is imagined as the messenger between the lover and the distant beloved. The final verses (20.15–20V) revert to the theme of the traveling yogis that occupies much of the two preceding *surs*. The name of this *sur* (S. *pūrabu* "the east") relates to the Gangetic region that is the home of the yogis (compare 20.19).

1 A reference to the skill of crows in bringing messages.

2 A place in Balochistan, to the west of Sindh.

21 Karayal

The rare Sindhi word *kārāyalu* (from S. *kāro* "black") is the name of a wonderful bird. The *sur* is largely devoted to praise of the wild geese (S. *hanja*), sometimes translated as "swans," which in Indian poetry are taken to symbolize the holy saints who have come to understand the value of the spiritual truths that are in turn symbolized by the jewels the geese find at the bottom of the lake. They are contrasted with the cranes that stand for those who are still immersed in worldliness, and with the hunters who represent those hostile to the values of the saints.

1 Compare 1.1.

2 The attraction of the lotus for the bee is a traditional poetic image for the power of love.

3 I.e., death, or the lower self.

4 The deadly power of the snakes who are the enemies of the wild geese is the subject of the final verses of this *sur* (21:14–19).

5 The reference is a legend in which the snakes that infested the jungle surrounding Junagarh were destroyed by yogis with their magical powers.

22 Sarang

Sarang (S. *sārangu*) is both the name of a musical mode associated with the rainy season and a word meaning "the rains," thus implying the romantic associations attributed to the season in Indian poetic culture. In this *sur* the monsoon rains are conceived of as a manifestation of divine power both in Sindh, where the appearance of the normally dry countryside is transformed by the rains, and across the rest of the world.

1 The rain bird (S. *tāṛo*, like the Hindi *cātak*) is a kind of cuckoo particularly associated with the rains. Compare 15.73.

2 Brides wear red at their wedding, and the color of the lightning is often described as red.

3 The universality of the divine blessing of the rains is underlined by this reference to the holy tomb of the Prophet in Medina.

4 In the Rajasthan desert to the east of Sindh.

5 The land immediately to the east of Sindh.

6 Meaning the lines of lightning in the sky; compare 22.6.

7 Kirar is the name of a depression near Shah Latif's place of residence at Bhit. It fills with water in the rainy season.

8 The numerous local place names in 22.20–22 evoke the spread of the rains, like the much broader spread of names in 22.38.

9 The association of the rainy season with love is underlined by the close verbal similarity in Sindhi between *mīṉhuṉ* "rain" and *nīṉhuṉ* "love."

10 The graceful gait of the elephant is proverbial.

11 The redness of the beloved's lips is compared to the color of the lightning; compare 22.18.

12 Here it is the yellowness of saffron that stands for the lightning that the beloved causes to flash.

13 The first month of the rainy season in the Indian calendar, corresponding to July–August.

14 A place in Sindh.

15 In Gujarat to the east of Sindh.

16 The verse evokes the spread of the rains sent by God to most parts of the Islamic world and beyond, later focusing on nearer places, like Girnar in Gujarat, Jaisalmer and Bikaner in Rajasthan, and Bhuj in Kachchh, before coming to the Dhat desert and the city of Umarkot in Sindh itself. The final invocation of God's blessings on Sindh is one of the most often quoted verses of the *Risālo*.

17 Meaning that the hoarders would make a 300 percent profit.

23 Rip

As indicated by the title (S. *ripa* "trouble, grief"), the predominant tone of the *sur* is one of lamentation.

1 The first of a series of striking images presented in the following verses.
2 Meaning, women living on their own without their husbands.

24 Barvo Sindhi

A Sindhi variant of the Indian musical mode Barva, the *sur* contains humble expressions of devotion to the beloved.
1 The image of the flute lamenting its original severance from the reed bed recalls the famous opening verse of Rumi's *Masnavī*: Pers. *bishnav az nai chūn shikāyat mīkunad, az judāīhā hikāyat mīkunad* "Listen to the lament of the reed flute, as it tells the story of separations."
2 Ar. *wa-tawāṣū bi'l-ḥaqqi wa-tawāṣū bi'l-ṣabri* (Qur'an 103.2), literally, "And join together in the mutual teaching of truth, and of patience and constancy."
3 The bitter apple (S. *ṭohu*) looks attractive but tastes bad.
4 Literally, "In the name of God," the Arabic phrase uttered to welcome any auspicious act.
5 Needed to measure out the grave that is to be dug.
6 I.e., were marked as his personal property.

25 Kapaiti

As indicated by the title (S. *kāpāitī* "spinner"), the *sur* deals with the popular theme of girls engaged in spinning, which is also commonly used as an image for proper conduct of human life by other Sufi poets, like Bullhe Shah (compare Shackle 2015: xx–xxi, 3–7, 293–319). The passing of human generations is symbolized by the continual generational turnover of young women. Those who are too lazy or arrogant to spin properly are criticized for their pride and idleness, while those who perform well are promised their reward when the thread they have spun is finally assessed at its true price by the divine dealer in cotton.

26 Piribhati

The familiar Indian mode Prabhati (S. *piribhātī*, Hindi *prabhātī*) is sung before dawn (S. *piribhāti*). Through the image of a sleeping musician, it is here linked to the Sufi theme of the continual need for awareness and for avoidance of heedless slumber.
1 As often in Sufi poetry, "tomorrow" (S. *subhāṉ*) indicates the time of judgment that follows death.

2 A ruler of Las Bela, to the southwest of Sindh proper, who was legendary for his lavish patronage of musicians. As throughout the following verses, the name of Sapar is invoked as a symbol of the infinite generosity of God.
3 Epithet of Sapar.
4 Sapar's undiscriminating munificence stands for the all-embracing quality of divine mercy.
5 The gift to a musician of a fine Arab horse is one of the most famous instances of Sapar's generosity.
6 Another epithet of Sapar.
7 The name of a musical mode performed in the early morning (S. *vihāgu*; compare Hindi *bihāgṛā*).
8 Ar. *wa-tu'izzu man tashā'u wa-tudhillu man tashā'u* (Qur'an 3.26), addressed to God. Compare 1.42.

27 Sorath

The title is the name both of a musical mode and of the woman Sorath (S. *soraṭhi*), who was the wife of Rai Diyach, the ruler of Junagarh in Gujarat. Anirai, the ruler of a neighboring kingdom, also wished to marry her. When his attack on Junagarh failed, Anirai offered a rich reward to anyone who would bring him the head of Rai Diyach. The challenge was taken up by the musician Bijal, who came to Rai Diyach and successfully demanded the latter's head as a reward for his performance.

Sorath is not the heroine of this *sur*, which instead focuses on the demand for supreme self-sacrifice on the part of Rai Diyach. Whereas the superficially similar story of the generous ruler Sapar is used in the preceding *sur*, Piribhati, to symbolize divine beneficence, Rai Diyach here represents the Sufi seeker who is required to give up everything, even his life, in his mystical quest. The *sur* was the subject of a pioneering scholarly study in German (Trumpp 1863), mainly focused on its linguistic features.

1 Ar. *ḳhalīlu 'llāh* "the friend of God," title given to the prophet Ibrahim.
2 Ar. *nārun ḥāmiya(tun)* "a fire blazing fiercely" (Qur'an 101.8).
3 Ar. *jannātu 'adnin* "gardens of perpetual bliss" (Qur'an 13.23).
4 Ar. *anā aḥmadu bilā mīmin* is a Hadith frequently quoted by the Sufis, which proclaims the close relationship between God and the Prophet. In the Arabic script, the word Ahad (احد) "the One," i.e., God, is distinguished from the name Ahmad (احمد), i.e., the

prophet Muhammad, only by the letter *mīm* in its very small medial form (-*m*-).

5 Ar. *al-insānu sirrī wa-anā sirruhu*, another favorite Sufi Hadith. Compare 3.4.

6 The royal fort of Junagarh.

7 I.e., the idea that the king must sacrifice his life to Bijal.

8 The sense seems to be that people are ready to sacrifice themselves in pursuit of their selfish desires, in contrast to the supremely selfless sacrifice Diyach is ready to offer.

9 Because of her son's noble generosity.

10 As a Rajput princess, Sorath would have committed suicide on her husband's funeral pyre after his death.

28 Dahar

Dahar is a Sindhi musical mode. The contents of the *sur* revolve around the themes of the transience of worldly existence and of yearning for the divine beloved. It consists of a series of quite loosely linked sections.

1 The verses in this first section (28.1–6) are developed around the Sindhi word *ḍhoru*, the dried-up course of a former branch of the Indus, once the site of bustling trade but now reclaimed by the desert where only thorn trees grow, following one of the many shifts in the historic route of the river. The Jasodhos were the former lords of this territory.

2 A common plant growing wild in the Indus valley.

3 The name of a former branch of the Indus.

4 This next section (28.7–11) is based around the fate of the big fish (S. *machu*) that has left it too late to avoid its fate at the hands of the fishermen.

5 The prophet Muhammad. This section of the *sur* (28.12–33) contains appeals for assistance from the divine beloved.

6 As often, the prince loved by Sasui stands for the divine beloved.

7 This section (28.21–33) moves from entreaties to the beloved to the familiar Sufi theme of the need for continual vigilance.

8 I.e., the world.

9 A new section (28.34–46) begins here, developing the themes of longing for the beloved and the transience of the world through a traditional Indian poetic image. The crane (S. *kūṉja*) comes to Sindh as a winter migrant. Its plaintive cry is thought to be an expression of pain caused by its separation from the flock.

10 The "wealthy herdsmen" (S. *sanghāra*) are invoked as protectors in this short section (28.47–50).
11 The day on which offerings are traditionally presented at Sufi shrines.
12 The verses in this final section (28.51–55) relate to Lakho Phulani, a legendary bandit from the heroic age of Sindh, who is remembered for his fearless attacks on the ruling Jarejo Samos. Here he represents the irresistible challenge of death.
13 The name of a wealthy tribe.
14 Ar. *kullu nafsin dhā'iqatu'l-mauti* (Qur'an 3.185, 29.57). Compare 5.67V, 14.64V.

29 Bilaval

Bilaval is a well-known Indian musical mode. The bulk of the *sur* (29.1–24, 29.35V) consists of verses apparently in praise of Jakhiro, a Rajput ruler of medieval Sindh famous for his bravery and generosity, but to be understood as forming an extended panegyric to the prophet Muhammad. In keeping with the conventions of Indian praise poetry, Jakhiro is addressed by a variety of names and titles, e.g., the epithet Rahu (the "upholder of the realm"); his alternative name, Abro; his title, Jadam; and his tribal affliation as "the Samo."

A sharply contrasting tone characterizes the final section (29.25–34) in description of Shah Latif's disgraceful but devoted disciple Vagand. These remarkable verses demonstrate a sharp satirical humor otherwise absent in the *Risālo.*

1 In ritual preparation for eating.
2 Such rewards for virtue are of less importance than the union with the divine that is the ultimate goal.
3 An image for the superior status of Muhammad as compared with the other prophets.
4 The verse refers to a famous episode in the heroic legends of medieval Sindh, when the invasion by the Muslim emperor of Delhi, Sultan Alauddin (d. 1316), was resisted by Jakhiro, who took under his protection the women of his fellow Rajputs, the Sumiros.
5 Another reference to the special status of Muhammad among the prophets.
6 A sign of the lavish generosity of the ideal Rajput ruler.
7 The special status of the prophet Muhammad is again underlined.

See the introductory note to 27 for Anirai, the ruler who was the rival of Diyach.

8 A legendary Arab chieftain who is proverbial for his generosity throughout Islamic literature.

9 Ar. *fa-kāna qāba kausaini au adnā* (Qur'an 53.9), said of the Prophet's uniquely close approach to the divine presence.

10 Compare 29.8.

11 As throughout this sequence of verses, the contrast between Vagand's hopeless condition when he relies on his own efforts and the bounty he receives from his *pīr* is used to illustrate the helplessness of humanity without the divine beneficence manifested through the Prophet.

12 A place near Shah Latif's residence at Bhit.

13 Ar. *raḥmatuhu lil-'ālimīna*, an epithet of the Prophet.

30 Kedaro

Kedaro (S. *keḏāro,* connected with Skt. *kedāra-* "field") is the name of a musical mode associated with martial themes. In the general context of the *Risālo,* the subject matter of this *sur* is unusual in being based upon a key episode in early Islamic history, the battle fought in 680 at Karbala in Iraq between Husain, the grandson of the Prophet, and the army of the caliph Yazid. The powerful mythic associations of the martyrdom of Husain at Karbala have given rise to a very large body of devotional literature in South Asia, starting with the hugely popular *Rauzat ul Shuhadā* composed in Persian around 1500 by Husain Va'iz Kashifi. While the Husain cult is particularly associated with Shia Islam (Hyder 2006), the figure of the martyred imam has always had a far wider appeal. It therefore is not too surprising that this overtly Shia material should be included in the Sufi context of the *Risālo* (Schimmel 1979). The exceptional character of the *sur* has nevertheless caused some editors to have reservations about its authenticity. It is accordingly omitted without explanation from Kazi 1961 and is placed immediately before the set of apocryphal *surs* included at the end of Baloch 2012.

The story of Karbala is here treated in the customarily allusive style of the *Risālo.* It begins with verses describing how Husain and his followers set out from Medina at the beginning of Muharram, the first month of the Hijri year (30.1–10), and then goes on to an account of the battle itself (30.11–17). References to the "five holy ones" (Pers. *panjtan-e pāk*) of the Prophet's family, i.e., the Prophet himself; his daughter, Fatima, and son-in-law, Ali; and their sons, the Imams Hasan and Husain, appear in the following verses (30.18–35). These develop subsidiary themes, including some familiar episodes that are separately explained in the notes below, before the final celebration of Husain's heroic martyrdom (30.36–44V).

1 Ar. *allāhu 'l-ṣamad* (Qur'an 112.2).

2 The word "bridegrooms" (S. *ghoṭa*) evokes the image of martyrdom as the consummation of a marriage in death.

3 Here the reference is to Hasan's son Qasim, who was married to his cousin, Husain's daughter Fatima Kubra, just before the battle of Karbala.

4 The annual Ashura festival of Muharram 10, which celebrates the martyrdom of Imam Husain.

5 The treachery of the inhabitants of Kufa, who first promised Husain their support, then betrayed him on the battlefield, is described here and in the two following verses.

6 The appeal conveyed by the bird to the tomb of the Prophet in Medina is one of the traditional legends associated with the story of Karbala.

7 Husain's elder brother Hasan had died shortly before the battle of Karbala.

8 The arrival of Hur, a senior officer in Yazid's army, to join Husain's forces is a much celebrated incident in the story of Karbala.

9 Ar. *lā yukallifu 'llāhu nafsan illā was'ahā* (Qur'an 2.286).

10 Because it will be in such demand to dye the dark clothes of mourning.

11 Ar. *fī sabīli 'llāhi* (Qur'an 5.57).

GLOSSARY

AHMAD Alternative name of the prophet Muhammad

ALI ('Alī) Son-in-law of the prophet Muhammad, and father of Hasan and Husain

ARI JAM (Ārī J̈ām) Punhun's father, also used as a title of Punhun

ARICHO (Ārīcho) Fellow tribesman of Punhun

ARIYANI (Āriyāṇī) Descendant of Ari

BHAMBHOR City in southern Sindh where Sasui lived

DHAT (Ḍhaṭ) The homeland of the Marus in the Thar desert to the east of Sindh

GANJO Hill in southern Sindh marking the start of the pilgrimage to Hinglaj

HAMIR (Hamīr) Title of Umar

HARHO (Hāṛho) Mountain range in Las Bela

HINGLAJ (Hinglāj) Pilgrimage site in Balochistan

HÔT Punhun's tribal name

HUSAIN Grandson of the prophet Muhammad who was killed at the battle of Karbala

JUNAGARH (Jhūnāgaṛh) Capital of a kingdom in Gujarat

KECH Punhun's home country

LAS BELA (Las Ḇela) Coastal area bordering southwest Sindh

MALIR (Malīr) Homeland of the Marus

MANSUR (Mansūr) The great Sufi saint Mansūr al-Hallāj, who was martyred in Baghdad

MARU (Mārū) Marui's tribe; also used as the tribal name of her beloved, Khetsen

MUSTAFA (Mustafā) Title of the prophet Muhammad

PAB (Paḇ) Range of hills in southwest Sindh

RANO (Rāṇo) Royal title of Mendhiro

SAMO Ruling Rajput tribe to which both Tamachi and Jakhiro belonged

SAVAN (Sāvaṇ) The month of the rainy season corresponding to July–August

SUMIRO (Sūmiro) Ruling Rajput tribe to which Umar belonged

VANKAR (Vaṇkār) A wooded area in Las Bela

YAZID (Yazīd) Leader of the army that defeated Husain at Karbala

BIBLIOGRAPHY

Editions and Translations

Trumpp, Ernest. 1866. *Sindhī-literature: The Dīvān of Abd-ul-Latīf Shāh, Known by the Name of Shāha jo Risālo.* Leipzig: Brockhaus.

Qalich Beg. 1913. *Vaḏo Shāh jo Risālo.* Shikarpur: Pokardas.

Gurbakhshani, Hotchand Mulchand. 1979. *Risālo Shāh 'Abd al-Latīf jo, 'urf Shāh jo Risālo.* Hyderabad: Shah Abdul Latif Bhitshah Saqafati Markaz Kameti. Originally published as 3 vols. Karachi: the editor, 1923–1931.

Advani, Kalyan B. 1958. *Shāh jo Risālo.* Bombay: Hindustan Kitab Ghar.

Shahvani, Ghulam Muhammad. 1960. *Shāh jo Risālo.* Hyderabad: R. H. Ahmad.

Kazi, Imdād Ali Imam Ali. 1961. *Risālo (Paighām) Shāh 'Abd al-Latīf jo.* Karachi: Sindhi Adabi Board.

Advani, Kalyan B. 1976. *Shāh jo Risālo.* 2nd abridged ed. Karachi: Maktaba-e Ishaqiya. Online version prepared by Abdul-Majid Bhurgri dated December 2010, available at www.bhurgri.com.

Mirza, Mumtaz. 1994. *The Ganj of Shah Abdul Latif Bhitai.* Hyderabad: Bhitshah Cultural Centre Committee.

Baloch, Nabi Bakhsh Khan. 2012. *Shāh jo Risālo.* Karachi: Culture Department, Government of Sindhi.

Sorley, H. T. 1953. *Musa Pervagans.* Abderdeen: Aberdeen University Press.

Ayaz, Shaikh. 1963. *Risāla-yi Shāh 'Abd al-Latīf: Shāh 'Abd al-Latīf Bhiṭāī kā manzūm urdū tarjuma.* Hyderabad: Sindh University.

Kazi, Elsa. 1965. *Risalo of Shah Abdul Latif (Selections).* Hyderabad: Sindhi Adabi Board.

Jotwani, Motilal, ed. 1969. *Shāh Latīf kā Kāvya.* [Selected verses in Devanagari script, with Hindi translation by Manishankar Dvivedi]. New Delhi: Sahitya Akademi.

Agha, Muhammad Yaqoob, ed. and trans. 1985. *Shah jo Risalo, alias Ganje Latif.* 3 vols. Hyderabad: Shah Abdul Latif Bhitshah Cultural Centre Committee.

Allana, G. 1989. *Selections from the Risalo.* Karachi: Cultural Wing Education Department, Government of Sind.

Qadiri, Ayaz Husain and Vaqar Ahmad Rizvi. 1993. *Kalām-i Shāh 'Abd al-Latīf Bhitāī (Urdū nasrī tarjuma).* 4 vols. Islamabad: Pakistan Academy of Letters.

Khamisani, Amena. 2003. *The Risalo of Shah Abdul Latif Bhitai.* Hyderabad: Bhitshah Cultural Centre Committee.

Makija, Anju and Hari Dilgir. 2005. *Shah Abdul Latif: Seeking the Beloved.* New Delhi: Katha.

Smith, Paul. 2012. *Shah Latif: Selected Poems.* Campbells Creek, Australia: New Humanity Books, 2012.

Shah, Mushtaq Ali. 2014. *Shah Abdul Latif Bhittai: Mystic Melodies.* Bloomington, Ind.: Author House.

Other Sources

Advani, Kalyan B. 1970. *Shah Latif.* New Delhi: Sahitya Akademi.

———. 1971. *Sachal Sarmast.* New Delhi: Sahitya Akademi.

Ajwani, L. H. 1970. *History of Sindhi Literature.* New Delhi: Sahitya Akademi.

Akhund, Abdul Hamid, ed. 1993. *Bhitai, the Message of the Master: An Anthology of Commentaries on the Poetry of Shah Abdul Latif.* Bhitshah, Hyderabad: Shah Abdul Latif Bhitshah Cultural Centre Committee.

Allana, G., trans. 1996. *Four Classical Poets of Sind: Shah Inat, Shah Abdul Latif, Sachal Sarmast, Sami.* New Delhi: Sahitya Akademi.

Ansari, Sarah F. D. 1992. *Sufi Saints and State Power: The Pirs of Sind, 1843–1967.* Cambridge: Cambridge University Press.

Asani, Ali S. 2003. "At the Crossroads of Indic and Iranian Civilizations: Sindhi Literary Culture." In *Literary Cultures in History,* ed. Sheldon Pollock. Berkeley: University of California Press, 612–646.

Baloch, N. B. K., ed. 1963. *Miyen Shāh 'Ināt jo kalām.* Hyderabad: Sindhi Adabi Board. Revised 2nd edition 2010.

———. 2010. *The Life and Thought of Shah Abdul Latif Bhitai.* Karachi: Culture Department, Government of Sindh.

Behl, Aditya. 2012. *Love's Subtle Magic: An Indian Islamic Literary Tradition, 1379–1549.* New York: Oxford University Press.

Boivin, Michel. 2015. *Historical Dictionary of the Sufi Culture of Sindh in Pakistan and India.* Karachi: Oxford University Press.

Burton, Richard F. 1851. *Sindh, and the Races That Inhabit the Valley of the Indus.* 2 vols. London: Richard Bentley.

Ernst, Carl W. 1997. *The Shambhala Guide to Sufism.* Boston: Shambhala.

Hussain, Fahmida. 2001. *The Image of "Woman" in the Poetry of Shah Abdul Latif.* Trans. Amjad Siraj Memon. Karachi: Shah Abdul Latif Chair, University of Karachi.

Hyder, Syed Akbar. 2006. *Reliving Karbala: Martyrdom in South Asian Memory.* Oxford and New York: Oxford University Press.

Jhangiani, S. M. 1987. *Shāh 'Abdul Laṭīf and His Times (1691 AD to 1751 AD).* Delhi: University of Delhi.

Jotwani, Motilal. 1975. *Shāh Abdul Latīf: His Life and Work.* Delhi: University of Delhi.

———. 1996. *Sufis of Sindh.* 2nd ed. New Delhi: Ministry of Information and Broadcasting, Publications Division.

Lalwani, Lilaram Watanmal. 1978. *The Life, Religion, and Poetry of Sháh Látif.* 2 vols. Lahore: Sang-e-Meel. First published, 1889.

Lambrick, H. T. 1964. *Sind: A General Introduction.* Hyderabad: Sindhi Adabi Board.

Mayne, Peter. 1956. *Saints of Sind.* London: John Murray.

Mirza, K. F. [Mirza Qalich Beg]. 1980. *Life of Shah Abdul Latif Bhitai.* Hyderabad: Bhitshah Cultural Centre Committee.

Pannke, Peter. 2014. *Saints and Singers: Sufi Music in the Indus Valley.* Karachi: Oxford University Press.

Rizvi, Saiyid Athar Abbas. 1978–1983. *A History of Sufism in India.* 2 vols. New Delhi: Munshiram Manoharlal.

Sadarangani, H. I. 1987. *Persian Poets of Sindh.* Hyderabad: Sindhi Adabi Board.

Sayed, Durreshahwar. 1988. *The Poetry of Shah Abd al-Latif.* Jamshoro/Hyderabad: Sindhi Adabi Board.

Schimmel, Annemarie. 1962. "The Martyr-mystic Ḥallāj in Sindhi Folk-poetry." *Numen* 9: 161–200.

———. 1974. *Sindhi Literature.* Wiesbaden: Otto Harrassowitz.

———. 1976. *Pain and Grace: A Study of Two Mystical Writers of Eighteenth-Century Muslim India.* Leiden: Brill.

———. 1979. "The *Marsiyeh* in Sindhi Poetry." In *Ta'ziyeh: Ritual and Drama in Iran,* ed. Peter J. Chelkowski. New York: New York University Press, 209–221.

———. 1981. "Shah Abdul Latif's Sur Sarang." In *Sind Through the Centuries,* ed. Hamida Khuhro. Karachi: Oxford University Press, 245–251.

———. 1982. *As Through a Veil: Mystical Poetry in Islam.* New York: Columbia University Press.

Shackle, Christopher. 1981. "Styles and Themes in the Siraiki Mystical

Poetry of Sind." In *Sind through the Centuries*, ed. Hamida Khuhro. Karachi: Oxford University Press, 252–269.

———, ed. and trans. 1985. *Hasham Shah: Sassi Punnun*. Lahore: Vanguard.

———, ed. and trans. 2015. *Bullhe Shah: Sufi Lyrics*. Cambridge, Mass. and London: Harvard University Press.

———. 2022. "Beauty on the Brink of Death: The Story of Sohni Revisited." In ed. Francesca Orsini. New Delhi: Oxford University Press.

Sindhi, Meman Abdul Majid, ed. 1962. *Karīm jo kalām*. Sukkur: Islamia College.

Sorley, H. T. 1966. *Shāh Abdul Latīf of Bhit: His Poetry, Life and Times* [including extensive translations from the *Risālo*, 297–420]. Lahore: Oxford University Press. First published 1938.

Syed, G. M. 1996. *Shah Latif and His Message*. Trans. Egbert Azariah. Sehwan Sharif: Sain Publishers.

Trumpp, E. 1863. "Eine Sindhī Sprachprobe: Sōraṭhi." *ZDMG* 17: 245–315.

———. 1872. *Grammar of the Sindhi Language*. London: Trübner.

Yusuf, Zohra, ed. 1988. *Rhythms of the Lower Indus: Perspectives on the Music of Sindh*. Karachi: Government of Sindh, Department of Culture and Tourism.

Yusuf Ali, A., trans. 1977. *The Holy Qur-an: Text, Translation and Commentary*. 2 vols. Lahore: Sh. Muhammad Ashraf.